Get Up and Groove!

Get Up and Groove!

Step Into Greatness (Perform)

Joey L. Dowdy

To order additional copies of this book, contact:
Xlibris LLC
1-888-795-4274
www.Xlibris.com
Orders@Xlibris.com
543879

CONTENTS

Motivational Movement Techniques

Book 1.

Where Dancespiration Meets Tranformation! True Motivational Stories of Real People Who Took The Step, and Made the Change, That Led Them to Transform Their Lives.

Famed Choreographer/Instructor/ & Fitness motivator Joey L. Dowdy motivational movement techniques will inspire, uplift, and teach you how to "Put Your Groove Into Action." You'll be sure to get hooked in learning how to Exercise Your Mind, Stimulate Your Body, and Elevate Your Soul.

ACKNOWLEDGEMENTS

Honestly, there are so many people to thank for this book I don't know where to start. So, let me start at the beginning. I want to thank my heavenly Father, the great creator, in which all things were made. I thank him for all his wonderful divine influences, and for giving me the gifts to do what I so love to do.

Next I want to thank my earthly mother and father for their loving embrace and continuous encouragement that taught me to "Never Give Up." I also want to thank all my handsome brothers and lovely sisters for their unwavering belief in me and kind words of wisdom.

I'd like as well to thank all my performer friends, students, clients, and supporters, who've always stood by me throughout the years. Your reassuring support has always kept me revved up to face life's many challenges. *I Thank You All.*

I'd also like to pay homage to every dance, singing, and / or acting teacher I've ever studied or trained under, and the brilliant instructors at world renowned **"Point Park University."** You guys were the backbone and strength that helped to mold me into what I've become today. *I Thank You.* Also here's a big warm shout out of **"Thanks"** to every dance studio or fitness center I've worked for with special thanks to Dennis & Sandy Potaro **(Athletic Garage Dance Center)**, George Latimer and Jeffrey Stuart **(Tennessee Ballet Academy)** Richard & Valerie **(Raskins Dance Studios)**, Bill & Lorraine Aubin Pennell **(Encore Dance Theatre)**, Jackie's Dance Studio, Mike & Dottie Tet **(Starlight Studios)**, **The Edge**

Dance Center, Millenium Dance Complex, Bally's Total Fitness & Bodies In Motion Centers. *I Thank You All For The Work.*

I would also like to thank my good friend **Henry Hirsch** who's so gifted and talented for his proof reading and special reflections work. You made the difference with this body of work. *Thank You!*

Last but not least, I'd like to thank you, **"Yes You,"** the reader. I thank you for deciding to take the step and make the change to finding your **"Greatness!"**

Groove ON!
J...

FOREWORD

Are you tired of sitting around every day thinking about, feeling, and doing the same old boring things? Which often leads to you getting nowhere? If so, it's time for a new direction and change. It's time to get your Mind in Gear and Your Body in Motion. It's time to "Get Up & Groove!" This book under my instruction will help you do just that by showing you how to "Put Your Groove Into Action."

Please allow me to introduce myself, I'm Joey L. Dowdy. I will be your narrator and personal guide. I am so excited to share with you my unique principles and techniques that I've assembled together from many years of being a professional Dancer, Performing/Artist, Choreographer, Instructor, and fitness motivator. Let me just say, I feel so fortunate and thankful to be able to do what I love, as well as love what I do.

My goal is to help others, just like you, learn how to do the same. It's to help you find, love, and live your passion towards a fulfilled life. Why? It's because far too often I witness people who are bound by limits and are living way below their capabilities.

Yet what astounds me is they don't even realize it. They don't seem to realize the only limits that exist are the ones they've created for themselves.

So that's where I come in; I want to help them discover and reach their fullest potential. That's what "Get Up & Groove Motivational Movement techniques" book series is all about. It's about taking control of your life through the exploration of movement and its many active methods.

The first book of the series is entitled, "Step Into Greatness! Perform!" It's where Dancespiration Meets Transformation, true stories of real people who took the step and made the change that led them to transform their lives. So if you're looking for a "Groove to Improve" your life this book leads the way to infectious inspiration that will make you, "Get Up Out of Your Seat and Start Grooving On Your Feet!"

SUPERSIZE
YOUR
MIND,
Not
Your
Portion
Size; Feed
It
Good
Nutritious
Brain
Food!

Exercise Your Mind
(The Supersize Effect)

Start Here; Go There

Did you know that the mind is a creative resource? As well, did you know every tangible thing that exists today came from the creation of someone's mind? Meaning, it therefore began with a thought. Why do I ask these questions? Well, if you're like most people, you probably go about your daily life never thinking about it. It might not have crossed your mind that the computer or laptop you work on, the I-pod or I-pad you use, the car you drive, the clothes you wear, the food you eat, or the chair that you're sitting in reading this, all started with a thought. It was a thought that someone, somewhere, envisioned one day becoming a reality.

For finding success in life, it first starts with the thought of knowing what it is you want. Yes, it all starts with you thinking about it. It's about the ability to be able to visualize yourself achieving your goals. It's a process I call, "Exercise Your Mind." Meaning, it's about putting your mind to good use. Because it is always ready, willing, and waiting to be utilized.

Store It

Here's what else. It's said that the brain, unlike the body, reaches a maturity level at an early age. Most statistics say it's before the age of eight years old. Which you must admit is quite astounding. Another captivating thing is how the brain is also recognized as "The Great Recorder." Meaning, it's known to keep a permanent record of everything we think, see, hear, feel, smell or touch.

Wow, I say that's pretty awesome too. Don't you think? It's so cool to know that it keeps a record of everything we've ever conceived in a safe place like a mental storage. So, it's no question that the brain is a fascinating and amazing part of the human anatomy.

Live the Call

Yet like I said earlier, the brain is known to mature at an early age. Thus, this is where our life's course and direction begins. It's at a tender young age when we start learning how to Exercise Our Minds.

And for me, I remember early on how that process began. It was through the joy of learning, which is a big part of my life, and has always kept my brain stimulated.

Okay, now, here's how my journey began. It all started when I was a kid around five or six years old. I remember being quite impressionable; especially by the things I heard. They really had an effect on my thinking, because I accepted most things I heard to be true.

I would say particularly the things that came from adults, like my parents, or teachers, who I so seriously respected. I remember how I literally took everything they said to heart. There is no doubt that their thought provoking influences had the biggest effect on me. It's odd now when I think about it. But I was so intrigued by their influence and mannerisms that they somehow seemed to sink into my subconscious.

I really didn't realize until a little later on in my life how much they affected me, as well as others. How so? They influenced me to develop similar characteristics of my own. These were strange, non-kid like behavior patterns that seemed to inspire me to start taking action for myself at a young age. Here's what happened.

My brothers and sisters used to tease me about being such a serious kid, stating they couldn't believe how early on in life I developed such a passion for discipline. But what surprised them was how unexpectedly these adult like mannerisms seemed to take place. They thought it was unusual how they showed up and were in full force even during what was supposed to be playful, kid-like moments. You know, doing things like playing games, playing around, or goofing off pulling pranks, and/ or playing practical jokes. These were all supposed to be fun, normal, and likeable kid's stuff. Well, they were for most kids!

Nonetheless for me, this wasn't so true. You see, it wasn't that I didn't want to have fun like everyone else. I did, but often my adult-like nature would take over. It seemed as though a different force to do things in a more practical way was controlling me. This was puzzling, and it made them wonder why I couldn't be a normal, free-spirited kid just like everyone else. They thought, "Why does he always feel the need to act like a little miniature adult? Why does he take everything so seriously?"

They said it was weird during these playful incidences how I positioned myself. It was known that you'd find me somewhere in the mix trying to organize, or rearrange things in a more suitable and sensible adult like manner. Yep! It didn't matter what it was. Even if it was a simple game of hide and go seek, they could always count on me to be the one in charge or the ringleader. They recall it was a natural occurrence for them to see me strategically placing, and or telling, kid's (much like a choreographer) to go here and there. They said, it wasn't in a demeaning or belittling way; yet for me it was serious business. Wow, how funny is that? I find it to be so surprisingly funny, that it makes me want to burst out with laughter every time I think about it.

What concerns me is how I never saw myself that way. I never knew I acted like such a serious kid. That explains why I literally took everything to heart. Here's what else I find interesting: I guess there's inevitably a "Call of The Wild." What I mean is, the future instructor side was speaking and being channeled through me. Maybe it's why

I so vividly remember one incident that possibly led me to answer this call.

Go For The Change

What was it? It was something that happened later during my early teen years. It was a reaction I had to a public service announcement or slogan that I heard on the radio, entitled "A mind is a terrible thing to waste" supporting the United Negro College Fund. Somehow hearing this message had a dramatic effect on me. How so? It captured my attention, and made the wheels of my mind spin out of control every time it aired. Why was this?

Well, that's the ironic part. I felt their message was totally inappropriate, demeaning, and a bit over the top. Please, let me explain. For one, I couldn't believe they used words in it like "terrible" and "waste." I thought to myself, "How dare they be so judgmental, bold, and harsh."

For instance, I thought the judgmental part was their assuming this would happen to every kid. Also, I totally disliked them using the word "terrible" because it sounded so bold and brass. And I couldn't believe they had THE NERVE to use the word "waste." Why? It bugged me because it's something I constantly heard my parents say I should never do.

So as you can see, that commercial totally didn't fly with me. In fact, it annoyingly got under my skin. Each time I heard it, it gave me a creepy feeling, as well as a deep sense of conviction. It felt like the UNCF was spying on me. It seemed as though they knew something about me that I didn't. And boy, I was starting to feel the discomfort through every fiber of my being. It was like their commercial was purposely being directed towards me.

However, here's the trick: let the truth be told, it *was* directed towards me. In fact, they did know something about me that I didn't. So, yes, it was aimed towards me in the sense that it was their secret weapon. Yet their targeted aim was for a good reason. Why? They knew sooner or later it would hit the bull's eye, and rouse up some unruly lad. Therefore it would cause him to take notice, and hopefully, action. Little did I know this lad would be me, and that their message would bring about a change I had no idea was coming.

No More Bullying

As I mentioned earlier, this happened during my early teen years. This was when I had a longing to be one of the tough boys, or as they were better known, "homeboys", "posse", or "entourage." Yes, the rebellious bullying type who thought they knew it all. Yeah, the ones who liked starting trouble simply because it's supposed to be a "cool thing to do." I'm sure you must have known a few cats like them yourself? Wouldn't you say?

Now here's the thing. In all reality, their so-called cool personas, and bullying ways, were nothing more than just a way for them to stand out. The surprising thing was they had no clue that, truthfully, their bad boy mentality was a reflection of their insecurities. It was more or less a cry for help; or a camouflaged call for attention. I'll go a step further; it was a disguise for hiding behind what they really desired the most. What was it? It was the need to feel accepted.

Yes, I too felt this need, which I guess made me no different from any other teenager who was seeking their own identity, as well as the answer as to what that really meant. All I knew is what it meant for me, at the moment, was I wanted to be cool and likeable too. So, I joined this one particular bully boy group simply because they appeared to have "it going on." Or so I thought!

Until one day something inside of me changed. It was after I had been with them for a while that I discovered things weren't as they seemed. What was different? I realized hanging out with my homeboys wasn't as appealing as it was in the beginning. Here's why. For one, I realized the bullying thing did nothing for me. Why didn't it? To me it seemed mindless - as though I was getting nowhere. Here's another reason. I was more of a shy and soft-spoken kid who didn't like being loud and unruly like my homeboys. Nor did I like to participate in rowdy events or violent acts like punking or pulling pranks on people, breaking into the school, gambling, missing school or getting into trouble.

Unlike my posse, I didn't have a problem with making new friends at school, my teachers, or even learning. Actually, I enjoyed them all. I especially liked to learn; it gave me such joy. I liked being able to share what I learned with others. In fact, maybe being bit by the learning bug is what made me decide to do what came next. What was it?

I decided one day, out of the blue, not to hang out with my homeboys. For some reason I felt compelled to rush home and get an early start on a particular homework assignment. I can't remember exactly what the assignment was, but it was obviously something that really intrigued me. I was all jazzed up about it until I realized there was possibly one teeny weenie problem that stood in my way. What was it, you might ask?

It was that I had to deliver this daunting news to my homeboys, who I knew would not take the news lightly, because it was after school when things with us really started to rock and roll. Just like school, we had our own scheduled assignments, and you should know it had nothing to do with paper work. So you can imagine how I felt about having to relay the "Hot Off The Press" breaking news that I wouldn't be able to hang out with them. I knew it would be anything but touching, or a "tender moment."

When I confronted them it was just as I expected. They pitched a fit and resorted to calling me every unearthly name known to man - or boy. But I didn't care, I was for whatever reason geared up and excited about getting home to complete my homework assignment. So I graciously took my butt kicking, quickly sprinted home, and got busy. It was weird because I had a slight feeling my bullying days might be a thing of the past.

Rise to The Occasion!

Little did I know when I returned to school the next day that my life would take an unexpected turn! It all began the moment I stepped into the classroom, in which I was pleasantly surprised to see all my homeboys there. As you should know, for them, showing up was an event that didn't happen too often. Yet I was glad they did. We talked and joked around a bit before the class started. Then when it got under way, to everyone's surprise we were all of a sudden hit with some shocking news. What was it? Well, here it goes.

The teacher decided to collect the homework assignment, score it, and apply the work towards our grades. We were all very surprised because it was scheduled to be a regular homework assignment that we would review in class. It wasn't perceived to be a possible pop quiz, or a test. It totally caught everyone off guard. We were all confused and couldn't figure out what sparked her to make such an unexpected and dramatic move. "Had she lost her senses?"

Others asked, "Was this another one of her "teacher gone wild" moments?" You know, where she either gave us too much homework, or sprang forth with another unexpected pop quiz. Okay, now tell me, I know you must remember a few unexpected "teacher gone wild" moments yourself? Don't you?

Well anyway, during this stunning classroom extravaganza, I could tell people were not happy. How did I know? It was obvious from hearing all the moaning and groaning that took place.

You should have seen the array of disappointing looks on kid's faces that seemed to vary. Some kids appeared to be only slightly surprised. I'm guessing it was due to them having completed the assignment. While some others had more of an incredulous look like, "Oh brother, why is she doing this to me?" Thirdly, there were those who looked like dead ringers by the look of sheer horror on their faces; they had not completed their assignment. Which I must admit unfortunately included all the guys from my little entourage.

Nonetheless those who had their homework were requested to pass it forward. I felt bad for everyone; I too was shocked by the teachers' request to collect the work. Yet to be honest, it was a big sigh of relieve for me to know that I did finish the assignment. Hey! Hey! Hey! Hey!

But wait! That wasn't the only good thing in the mist of all this mayhem. Actually, there was something else. In fact, it was the one thing you could count on no matter how hectic your school day had been. It's something that would always help to ease the pain. What was it? I was the realization of knowing it was the last class of the day.

Oh! What a feeling. Do you remember? Well, if not, let me refresh your memory. It was a feeling of perpetual joy, or what I would call having a "Yahoo," or "Thank Heaven" moment. Why? Because like I said, it didn't matter how hectic the earlier part of the day went. All that mattered was that it was the last class of the day and soon we'd be on our way home, or wherever.

Shortly thereafter the bell rang, and everyone immediately leaped to their feet, as the teacher announced that class was dismissed. Then we all paraded towards the doorway to exit and take our rightful place out in the world.

However, as I was about to exit the room, the teacher asked if she could speak with me. I said, "Sure!" Just then my heart started beating so fast I thought it was going to jump out of my chest. It was a suspenseful moment that I'll never forget. The kind of spellbinding moment that will make your speech slur, hair stand up, and you almost wet your pants.

I'm sure you can relate; haven't you had one of those moments? As I continued I thought to myself, Oh boy! What have I done now? I couldn't believe that out of everyone leaving the room she chose to single me out. I mean, why was it so important for me to rise to the occasion?

Do the Work!

Then she said, "Joey, you're probably wondering why I asked to speak with you? I said, "Yes!" She continued, "I've been watching you for quite some time now; I admire your good work. I can tell briefly from looking at this assignment as well from some others, that you put time and effort into your work. I've noticed it is always quality. Sure, I'm aware you've had some days where you've missed some valuable class time. However, what I know is, when you do get focused and do the work, it's evident you go the extra mile. That is what impresses me most about you. It's exactly why I stopped you.

I see you as someone who has great potential. What I also like is you seem to have a strong desire to learn. I strongly believe if you continue to stay focused, committed, and keep working hard, you have the ability to succeed. I would even predict you could, one day, 'be somebody special.' It's possible you could go very far with your life, but there's a problem."

I responded by saying, "problem?" She said again, "yes, there's a problem. It's something serious, and it could possibly hold you back."

Then I asked, "What is it." Even though I couldn't believe I was having this surreal moment. Neither could I believe she was saying such things to me.

She continued by saying, "Joey, you're hanging out with the wrong crowd, honey." She said something too I didn't quite understand at the time stating, '*What won't grow you will slow you, meaning it could stop you from succeeding.*' 'It's all about the company you keep, and that group is not the best company for you. Did you notice how they didn't have their homework, but you did?" "Yes, I did."

Next she said, "It's apparent to me that your friends are not interested in learning, or in getting an education like you. I can tell, because I've given them many chances to '*rise up and meet the challenge.*' In spite of all my efforts I still hardly ever see them in my class; nor do they make any attempt to do the work. All I ask for is a little effort. So I think unless something dramatically changes the chances of them passing school, or making it successfully in life, looks very slim."

Okay, what she said next was so shocking that it made my spine tingle. She said, "It's a shame because, 'The mind is a terrible thing to waste.' However, you do stand a chance. Here's why, my child. Your eagerness to learn and willingness to do the work shows me that you do have a future, if you choose to pursue it. Therefore the time is now. Don't wait until it's too late."

Say Role Model!

Boy! All she had to say shocked me, yet I was amazed - and excited too - that she saw such potential in a little insecure brat like me. Why? It's because this wasn't just your ordinary teacher. Well, at least it didn't seem that way to me. I saw her as a role model and the ultimate professional. Sure, I admit, she was tough. Yet, what I really liked about her was how she had no favorite student and treated everyone fairly. This is why I think she was so highly respected. Miss Teach, (well, this is what I'll be calling her in slang words of course) was always on her game. Especially when it came to getting the job done; her passion and commitment showed she was a lady about her business.

You could tell because she was always fired up, prepared, and ready to get grooving. Which were all unique qualities and characteristics that so many of us little bratty students lack, yet we so desperately needed. That's why her fan base of student followers had such admiration for her. We liked how she was poised and confident; I mean this lady really knew how to carry herself. For instance, when it came to being poised and demonstrating good posture, it seemed like she wrote the book. It was evident that she practiced these things because it showed whenever she was standing or sitting.

Yeah, you would never catch her sitting all slouched over like most of us teens did. It's the sort of thing that makes you laugh when you realize her stance exemplified everything your mom would tell you to do. These were such things as, "please sit up straight and don't slouch over, now, lift that chin and pull back those shoulders."

Another thing, when it came to her displaying confidence, there was definitely nothing lacking in that area either. Her persona shined through like a new coin in many ways - her smile, eye contact, and stylish dress, for instance. These too were all things we teens carefully took note of, as this was one vital area that many of us needed to work on.

Here's what else stood out. It amazed me how you could tell she was always herself. Unlike us teens, she never came across as trying to be someone she was not. It was a lesson learned for all of us. This is what I mean. Teenagers are big imitators who are always trying to mimic and be like someone else. Here's what's so surprising, who would have thought that even Miss Teach had a few imitators of her own? In which I will talk more about that later. Yes, Miss teach's ability to be herself had a dramatic effect on many.

It so reminds me of a great neo-soul singer named India - Arie, who sings a dynamic, uplifting, and self -awareness inspiring song called, "Just Do You!" from her album entitled "Songversation". It's a very bouncy and danceable song about the importance of always being who you are. Now, what's great about it is I could see this song being played as Miss. Teach life's sound track every time she walked into a room.

Because, boy, when she walked into a room everybody took notice. It didn't matter if it was the classroom or the cafeteria. Oh yeah! Remember? The cafeteria is a place where everyone was supposed to be on his or her best behavior, sit down, and quietly eat their lunch. Nonetheless, we all know this wasn't the case. Somehow this hourly gathering became a place I called, "Funsville Eatery." It was more like a place that suggested an hour of much needed freedom. Meaning, it became less secluded and more of a place for us to escape to, where we could get away from the drudgery of having to sit and think for long hours. Well, actually, we still sat but it was a different kind of rump sitting. It was fun rump sitting where we didn't have to think about anything educational if we didn't want to. Sure, there was plenty of food to eat, and we filled our bellies. But that wasn't the only good reason why we rushed through the hallway, when the lunch bell rang, trying to get there. We knew once we did, that there would also be excitement and adventure. Yes! Spending an hour at Funsville Eatery meant we could sneak in a few good laughs, goof off, play around, or indulge in overly loud conversations just to see who could attract the most attention.

Remember? Okay, now back to Miss Teach. In spite of all the cafeteria hoopla there was still something about her that made you want to look over when she walked into the room. It's because she didn't just walk into a room; she made an entrance. It was like she owned her space in the room, in fact, it was apparent that she knew how to work the room. She did it so well that even her imitators were eye balling every move she made. Why were they?

Like I mentioned earlier, teenagers are big imitators who are always trying to mimic or be like someone else. So, yes, Miss Teach was no exception; she too had quite a few imitators. These were usually kids who loved to make fun of her walk, which they did on different occasions. You'd see them lined up one by one trying to duplicate it. Here's why.

She had a forceful, firm, and unhesitant kind of walk. Actually it appeared to be more like a strut or stride. The puzzling thing was I could never figure out how she did it in high heels. Hey, was she related to "Strut," the girl in one of my other stories? Here's what else. You always knew when Miss Teach was approaching because you could hear the clicking and clacking of her pumps a mile away. When she walked it was as though her steps were always strategically placed. It was much like a super model working and walking down the runway with one foot crossing in front of the other. Yeah, it was exactly like Strut!

I remember too, we being kids of course, how we jokingly laughed and closely observed her in hopes of just maybe one day she'd teeter over in those high heels. Or that she might possibly lose a heel, or anything, so we could get in a good chuckle. But to our surprise she never did.

Wait! You must know the fun didn't stop there. We also made light of her proper, precise, and very clear diction. As well as her "snazzy dress for success" attire and philosophy that wasn't just something she talked about, but lived to a tee.

Furthermore, in spite of all that, what I really think made her such a stand out and admired teacher was the way she connected with her students. It was her tough love, and positive words of wisdom and encouragement that made the difference. As well as the "you can do it" gleam in her eyes that seemed to pierce right through you whenever she spoke. These were all outstanding characteristics that made her a role model, and distinctly different from the other teachers.

Complete The Puzzled

I couldn't believe it when she looked directly into my eyes and quoted the phrase from the PSA "A mind is a terrible thing to waste." It nearly blew me away. I admit it took my teen age thinking perspective to a new level; I honestly started to grasp what she was saying. I couldn't believe it was making sense to me. Her words made me see why it was important for me to get on the right track. It was like putting missing pieces from a puzzle back together again. Just like what Carla talks about in her "Lean, Mean, Plus Size Dancing Machine" story. That's why I began to feel differently about hanging out with my homeboys. I knew in my heart it wasn't the best choice, the right fit, or direction for me.

Waste Not!

It now made sense to me why UNCF initially put out such a deliberately blatant message. Why did they? It was clearly a ploy; a plan they used to make me think. Yet they took it a few steps further by making it a call to action, it sent the wheels of my mind spinning. It made me realize that those little sneaks (UNCF) knew exactly what they were doing. It was a trick they knew sooner or later would get the attention of a few gullible kids like me.

Wow! How clever. It worked! Even though, I wasn't sure how Miss Teach knew.

It made me wonder, "Was she in on it too?"

That's why every time I heard that commercial it was as if it were poking at me. It really had me stirred up and made me think about my life's direction. It stuck to me like glue. I get why it felt like an awakening. It's because those words had power. In fact, now I know words in general have power. They have the power to lift you up, or tear you down, to make you smile, or to make you frown. Words simply have the power to "make you think, and can ignite you to take action," like what they finally did to me. Here's what else. Those powerful thought-provoking words put fear in me. Little did I know they were sinking into my subconscious mind. I was actually afraid

I could possibly turn out to be another wasted mind, if I didn't do something. That's exactly why I scurried home that day to complete my homework assignment.

It's also why I had a problem with the words "terrible "and "waste." It's because they seemed like bad words; the kind of words I didn't want to attach myself to.

Like I said before, my parents taught me and my siblings that wasting any thing was never good. They said, "Never take anything for granted (food, clothes, money, school) and use whatever you're been given, or blessed with, to its fullest." I thank them for as well instilling in me the importance of getting a good education. They told me it was the pathway that led to a promising future. They taught me that anything is possible to the thinker who educates himself and believes he can do all things. They said there were no limits for what one could achieve if he/she dares to dream big, and go forward in achieving it. They stated it would never be a waste of time, or effort, if you work hard, stay focused on your goals, and persevere through the ups and downs. These were the essential tools you needed to achieve inevitable success.

Plant Seeds For Success

I was amazed at how this incident confirmed my parent's theory. I thank them for planting in me their seeds of knowledge and wisdom. It is what I believe caught the teacher's attention, as well as taught me the value and importance of learning how to "exercise my mind." I saw it was something that should be used to its fullest. It was something too, that UNCF'S message did so brilliantly by planting their seed. I am thankful they did; and since then the seed has blossomed me into being the professional I always dreamed of becoming.

Now when I think back I realize that their message started taking root the day I decided not to hang out with my posse. It started a new movement shift and an internal soul search for my life's purpose and direction. It made me dig deeper, and the results were that I sprang forth to the top with what were once hidden dreams and goals. These were things I had only imagined, but never fully begun to explore until that day.

Therefore my teacher's kind thought provoking words of encouragement were the icing on the cake; her words grabbed my attention that day and haven't let go since. Yes! It was a defining moment that boosted my self-esteem and confidence to the next level. I started to believe in myself. She made me feel special and it opened my eyes to realize that I didn't need the support from an unruly group of guys to give me my source of strength, or to verify my being accepted. I accepted myself. I believed I could be an achiever.

Be Disciplined

Her words made me think. I thought, hey, maybe I really could be somebody one day. Maybe life could possibly have meaning and purpose. I felt I should take heed to what she was saying; as it was apparent to me that she really felt I could be somebody.

So, I got busy and started doing the work. Sure, I knew it wasn't going to be a piece of cake; it would be tough! However, I was willing to give it a try. And my first step was to immediately vacate the entourage, and so I did. I then struck out on my own in search of finding and fulfilling my new destiny. I knew it would require me to take a new direction and to make some different choices. My next step was to figure out what I wanted to do with my life- you know- what intrigued me! So I thought about it, what talents I had, as well as what I really wanted to pursue. Then I discovered that I loved the performing arts. I had dreams about one day doing it professionally, yet I wasn't sure if I could. What instilled in me the thought that I possibly could was the fact that I had participated in a few talents shows as a performer, in which I was told I had talent. In fact, I won several events. In addition I also took a few performing art classes in dancing, singing, and acting. It was fun and those teachers also told me that I had potential. So to me, what this meant was these were all incidences that showed I was definitely heading in the right direction.

I realized I had the confidence to do it, and from there on that I went full speed ahead. The ironic part was, it didn't take long before I was hooked. I loved the classes and the training. What I also realized was that the classes not only worked my body, but my mind as well. I learned that it's true; "You can't have an active mind with an inactive a body." This is what made me destined to be, and do, my best in pursuing my dreams.

On the other hand, it took sheer will power to resist the temptation after school to skip classes so I could go hang with my friends. You better believe it was difficult seeing them head out for soda or ice cream as I headed to the studio for a dance class, or a singing lesson, or to the rehearsal hall for acting class, or play practice. Anyway, what I did in order to keep a few friendships was, I compromised. I decided to do social things like that during my down time, or on a day off. Sure, I realized the importance of having a social life, but I also needed to stay focused on my goals as well. It was apparent that I was driven by determination and a much bigger vision. Honestly, I liked what I felt and the challenge it brought. I didn't mind the sacrifice, along with the blood, sweat, and tears it would take for me to achieve my dreams.

You bet it took a great deal of discipline, training, and hard work. It took a daily commitment. Nonetheless that was all fine and dandy with me, because I was on a mission. It was a personal mission. I deeply wanted to prove to myself that I could be somebody. Yet, there was one thing for sure I knew I didn't want to be. I didn't want to be another statistic. You know, another "wasted mind."

Follow Your Vision

When I look back, those were such defining moments in my life, and it was situations like those that gave me a reason to continue following my dreams. It truly opened my eyes and now I totally understand why the mind is a terrible thing to waste if you don't exercise it. It will remain inactive, unless you keep it active.

This is why I hope my story will inspire you to start activating your mind. Or maybe it has already. If so, how did the process come about for you? Perhaps it'll motivate you to share your story. Yes, your own story about what inspired you to start exercising your mind. But if not, don't worry. It's okay, if you're still in need to just find the motivation to "Get Up and Groove." Remember, 'It's Never Too Late!" You can start today. All you have to say is, "Out with the old and in with the new." How can you do this? It's simple. Make a fresh new beginning. Know that you have all the resources right here to help you create it. And let me tell you it's all about being creative. Why is it so important? Check this out!

Creativity, not convenience, is the king or queen who rules the day. You may not realize this, but it's also a mental and physical form of action and expression. It's what our world thrives on. No task driven idea put into fruition is too big or small if it produces results. It can make even the biggest skeptic see how powerful the use of the mind can be when it's even semi-active. How so? I think its evident today more so than ever. Just look around you. What do you see?

You'll see a big beautiful universe that's filled with endless possibilities. Think about it. Who would have thought a century ago what was once only someone's thought, idea, or dream would now a century or so later be turned into a full-fledged reality. Who would have thought we would be driving cars, motorbikes, buses, and traveling around the world on airplanes or trains? Who knew we'd also be using electrical gadgets like the telephone, computers, I-pads or I-pods. Or even have a machine that separates water from sludge and oil? Okay, do you want to know what's so unbelievable about these examples, and what following your vision can do for you? It's like this.

Endless Creation

Know that these are all amazing devices created by someone who had a hunch, an idea, a gut feeling, and the vision that this is what the world needed. Nonetheless they didn't stop there; it took applying themselves with a little elbow grease to eventually make their dreams become a reality. And I'm sure you can do the same. Just about anything is possible if you think so. That's why I love the phrase that says, "The person who says it can't be done is usually interrupted by someone doing it."

It's true. The key is to tap into your own creativity by using your mind. Remember: It can take you places where your body can't go. You can create a world for yourself full of whatever you imagine it to be. No! It's not impossible. Here's why! Great thinkers make good achievers who make great inventions just like the ones I mentioned earlier.

So, what are you waiting for? I bet you're on the **"Sit List."** What is it? It's something I will be talking more about in book two, but briefly, it's about sitting down on a few ideas that could not only make your dreams come true. They could as well as potentially make you a ton of moola. But more importantly they could have the unleashing power to do a world of good. Think about this; maybe you have a brilliant idea for curing world hunger, or a cure for Aids, Cancer, or Alzheimer's etc.? Or maybe it's simply about the need for you to reinvent your life, and/or create a fresh new start for yourself. Hmmm! Any and everything is possible if you dare to dream big. Now do you too see why the mind is a terrible thing to waste? There need be no waste; all you need to do is "Exercise Your Mind." It will be an investment well worth making.

Here's your **Mind in Motion Recap at Work, so** let's pull forward a few tips!"

- **Store It:** Know that what you desire to do is already stored away in your brain's mental storage box for safekeeping. Now, all you need to do is locate the right key that'll open it.
- **See a Vision For Yourself.** Find out what you like doing and go forward with it, and if you're not sure, experiment, be imaginative, use your skills and talents. Have fun!

- **Follow Your Gut Instinct:** It's never too early or late; any age is suitable for moving towards what feels natural to do.
- **Rise up! Meet the Challenge!** Don't be afraid to Step Up & Step Out. Do Something Extraordinary!
- **Go for Change:** Don't be afraid of trying something different if it enhances your life or makes you step out of your comfort zone.
- **Accept yourself** and believe you can be an achiever; know that you don't need validation from someone else to feel complete.
- **Learn Discipline:** It will teach you valuable lessons about structure, patience, perseverance and sacrifice.
- **Find a role model or a mentor:** Let it be someone who's a positive influence, someone you look up to and whom you can talk to who will support your brilliant ideas, or even nutty little plans.
- **Do the Work**: Remember - execution is the process for achieving your goals.
- **Hang Around** positive people, seek influences that'll help you grow, and keep your mind stimulated.
- **Waste Not:** Use every resource you come across to your advantage such as your schooling, job experience/ work, or personal connections.
- **Be Creative**: Think, be, and live creatively; know that creativity is the source from which all things come.

Soul in Motion Tip
Go Do It

*Find the one fun thing you like doing every day, then take a breath, and go do it.

Mind in Motion Tip
READ

*Spend some time reading. The key is to start reading what you like as long as it's productive (meaning don't just look at the pretty pictures!) and beneficial. However, if you're not used to reading much, or don't like to read, but know you need it (we all do!) I suggest you start with just fifteen minutes and then work your way up to thirty minutes per day of reading.

What you'll notice is how little by little it will become easier and more enjoyable. Then before long an- hour, or two- it will come with ease. Plus, reading has such great benefits. Like these:

It's very therapeutic;

It sharpens your mind.

It helps you develop a clearer speech.

It stimulates your muscle memory.

It intrigues your brain.

It expands your thoughts

It creates a visual world.

It takes your mind places where your body can't go.

It broadens your vocabulary.

Groove Theory: I know, for some people this may sound like a chore. However, I think the benefits will outweigh the small effort it takes. Don't forget that it's just like all other aspects of life even though sometimes it takes a minute to get going. But once you do, it's often well worth it. That's what I call **"The Supersize Effect."**

Half
   Stepping
      Will
         Leave
          You
           Behind,
  It Takes
       Full
         Steps to
          Get Ahead!

Strut!
In Six Inch Heels

Put Your Best Foot Forward

This could be considered a story in which an ugly duckling turns into a beautiful swan. Not so much with regard to looks, but rather a story about beating the odds when expectations may not be too hopeful. I remember meeting this girl for the first time when she was around the tender age of eleven or twelve. I'll call her "Strut." She auditioned for me when I was working as a choreographer for a kid's stage show called "Block Party." She was one of about fifty kids auditioning for the show. Strut was shy by nature but also a very sweet, eager, ready, and energetic little girl. When she started the audition, I could just tell from her warm smile and those big Bambi eyes, how this little girl had a deep desire to impress me.

I began by asking her what solo piece she was performing (it was required first before moving on to the next phase known as the "call back" round, in which, if approved, each performer would be given set choreography which showed if they could pick up fast and/or follow my lead). In a soft voice she answered, "I'm doing Janet Jackson's Rhythm Nation." Then I asked, "Can you work it like Janet?" She replied, "I will give it my best." Little did she know that I was rooting for her because I too was a devout "Janet" fan. So I said, "That's great! Okay! Now, let's see it."

Come to Life

I played the music and, "Oh Boy!" did Strut come to life. I mean she had all of Janet's moves down! Groove on this: *Your Mind In Motion Is Powerful, Like A Laser Beam Piercing Through the Toughest Object!"* I like how she beamed in on executing her moves with enthusiasm and authentic style. What really surprised me was how Strut managed to give them a more feminine touch, even in the midst of what seemed like an eclectic two-minute piece that was composed of musical mayhem and choreography that matched her sharp, hard hitting, and militant routine. All while she acted out the part with great facial expressions and sincerity.

In fact, her infectious, bubbly personality was so radiant that I believe it would have put a smile on that grumpy old man in "A Christmas Carol" - old man Ebenezer Scrooge's face. Another thing I liked about Strut's audition was how she dressed the part wearing the military hat, coat, and all. To me it proved that she wasn't just a dancer, but much like Janet, an actress as well. You could see she had diligently studied Janet as well as the role. Now she was geared up, and ready, to work the part. I would reference her performance much like what Alicia Key's referred to in one of her songs in which she said, *"This girl is on fire!"* And she certainly was.

What I liked most about her audition/performance routine was how her hot fiery flames gave off sparks that showed her versatility. How so? For one, her routine showed me that she had the ability to follow set choreography. Secondly, I liked how in certain sections, she added a few of her own unique signature moves. This proved to me she also had a sense of originality. And last but not least - there was something else: I couldn't help but notice her natural physical beauty, which just seemed to jump out at you. It's a fact that these are all great qualities that worked to her advantage, but here's the real kicker: Even though I liked what she was presenting. I think she might have, like a magic trick, pulled a rabbit out of a hat for some who didn't expect what came next.

Let me explain, as it was obvious to me from the looks on some of the more established performer's faces waiting to audition, that they never expected Strut could be a potential threat. I think they never expected her to be so good or impressive. Like I said earlier, "she really did light up." I believe in their eyes she seemed more like the underdog, rather than someone who might have real threatening talent. Why would I say this? It's because I noticed how they were a bit more reserved and even standoffish towards her in the beginning.

Kill It, or Chill It?

How did I know this? Here's how. Normally I like to do what I call "scout the room" before the audition starts just to check out the scene. I know from first-hand experience that many unusual situations and sometimes crazy, unpredictable moments happen before the audition starts. For example, some people let their nerves get the best of them. They simply can't handle the competitive pressure, so they end up talking themselves out of auditioning at all. Then there are other incidents, like people who get so overwhelmed with all the things to do before the audition that they end up blowing it. How so? They arrive at the audition and discover that they forgot to bring their picture and resume. Sound interesting? Wait! There's more.

There's another interesting thing I've noticed at auditions. What is it? It's that they certainly seem to attract every type of opportunist and /or character imaginable. "Like whom?" you might ask. Well, it's everybody from the amateur to the student in training, including people who believe that they don't need to train because they naturally have what it takes. And from my teaching expertise, believe me, today more so than ever, there is no shortage of this type of people. Then there are the professional performers, as well as those who are striving to be just like them. You can count on this group being the ones who are prepped, ready, willing, and waiting for the challenge. This would be the category Strut seemed to fit in. Her commitment and focus proved to me that she took this seriously. There was no doubt that she was on a serious quest, and it was evident that she might one day have her heart set on being a professional performer. What really amazed me too, was how much more relaxed and chilled-out she appeared to be; more than some of the others who were waiting for their audition.

Beware, Oh, What Yonder Lurks

This also made me wonder how she reacted when being approached by this next group of characters I call, "Audition Predators." Who are they, and what purpose do they serve? Audition predators are usually a small group of people who lurk around at auditions. Their main objective is to scope and try to psych out their competition. Their strategy is to approach select people who they feel could possibly be a threat to them and then put a little nervous fear, and/ or intimidation, under their feet. Or even perhaps scare them away so that they, the predators, stand a better chance of getting the job. Or so they think. *Does* it work? I would say, hmmm, sometimes. *How does it work?* Check this out. They often go up to the people they've selected during the audition process while they're practicing or getting ready. Then they will make a few sly remarks, thinking it might make them break their concentration. Or perhaps they'll say something to the person hoping it'll make them second-guess themselves about being right for the job.

For instance; they might say something like, "Well, you know, this audition is fixed; they already know who they want." They'll say this thinking it might discourage the person from trying. Or they might say to someone else in a "sly fox" manner before they go on to audition something like, "Have a good audition, and don't mess up" and hoping they'll hang on to the thought, and possibly do so. This classic incident happened to a close friend of mine; when she clung onto the thought, which resorted to her therefore messing up and blowing the audition.

Or you might hear them say to someone else something like, "Hey, they're only looking for tall people this audition because thus far all (referring to themselves as well) the short people have been getting cut. And if you happen to be short, and you're still waiting to audition, oh Brother! What's a girl or boy to think?

So, how do I know for sure these scenarios aren't just hearsay? It's because I've personally experienced similar situations. Okay, now here's what I find so interesting about this little group of instigators. I have often noticed how none of them ever seem to get chosen for the job. Nor do they even make the final cut. Could it be like what they say, "Their bark is bigger than their bite? "Or all they are is just a big ol` bag full of hot air?" My answer to both statements would be a definite "Yes!" However the question is what do you do when confronted by one, two, three, or more sneaks like them?

Here's what I say you do. I say you count to three, then get into your best preparatory position, and give them a fan kick (think "karate round house kick") like they'll never forget. You know - the kind that slightly brushes past their nose. Yeah, a kick like the one you see in the martial arts movies where it has so much power that if you're not aware of the danger that lurks, it could catch you off guard, as well as deliver what would seem like a breeze that lingers a while after it passes. Now doesn't that sound good?

Rev Up for the Race

Okay, Okay! You know I'm only joking. Plus, it wouldn't work as well because these characters are never physically violent. They're only about lip service. So that wouldn't be necessary, nor would it be the smartest tactic to use. This is what I really suggest you do. I suggest you beat them at their own little game.

How can you? Listen closely. What you do is turn the beat around, so that the psychology ends up being played out on them instead. Here's how. When they approach you, just smile and pretend like you're interested in what they have to say. What that will do is make them think you're under the spell of their sweet allure. Go ahead; just let them think you've been won over.

Next, whatever thoughts they try to impose upon you, just erase them from your mind. Yes, toss it into your invisible mental trash can. Now you're free to focus your thoughts, energy, and attention solely on your audition. Then use your imagination and pretend like you're a race car getting revved up for the big race. Once the flag drops (your audition number being called) put the pedal to the medal. Deliver a gas guzzling performance that'll leave tire marks all over the dance floor. Let them (the audition predators) see and smell the cloud of smoke you leave behind from a mile away. Therefore, once you make the cut, or even if you don't, you'll still feel good regardless - because you simply gave it your grandest try. Then your problem will be solved. Here's how you'll know. I can assure you that after you do this you can count on those Audition Predators to be nowhere in sight. This will mostly happen after they see you celebrating the victory of defeat because their little sneaky plan did not work. Psych! Okay, now getting back to the story...

So during my pre-audition room scouting, it was apparent to me that Strut was more of a loner because she wasn't all grouped up. I could see that she wasn't part of any click, or noticeable entourage. Neither did I see her being over exerted by doing what I call *"The Over Kill Sell."* What is it? It's trying to attract attention by practicing or performing rather unnecessary gymnastics and or gimmicky dance tricks that I believe really aren't necessary if you're not getting ready to try out for the Olympics. I mean, why over exert yourself when you should be saving your precious energy for the big event?

It's best to do this: "just chill out." I like how Strut took this approach. In fact, it was so cool to see how relaxed she was. She just simply found a peaceful corner of the room and did her prep work in a moderate, quiet, and respectful manner.

But what drew so much attention to her was the dramatic costume she wore. It really made her stand out. It made a statement that implied how she was dressed to impress. It was so unexpectedly different from what most other dancer/performers wore. Most were dressed in their more casually *stylish Danskin gear*, or other popular modest dance apparel. So you can imagine how Strut's look alone made her the topic of attention, as well as the recipient of frequent glares. I couldn't help but notice how some would look over at her as they passed by, then let out a giggle or two as if signifying their dislike as to what she was wearing. Remember? It's how kids can be sometimes. Nevertheless, I'm sure that what she wore made them curious as to what it was she would be performing.

It's because now all the wondering, waiting, and giggles were over. It was show-and-tell time. And this powerhouse performer was ready to take center stage and deliver. This she did indeed with an arousing audition/ performance that introduced her, and shocked some, like none other. I think it's amazing in life how sometimes the tide will turn in your favor. Especially, if you do what I believe always works. What is it? Its doing what I call, *"Let The Proof Be in The Pudding."* Meaning, Talk or even giggles can be cheap, so *"Let Your Actions Be Your Star Attraction."* It's about stepping up to meet the challenge, and then showing them what you can do. It is what will separate the "haves" from the "have nots." It will show, and the end result of your hard work will speak for itself. The lesson learned here is it's not necessary to do cartwheels, or back hands springs, if not needed, to get someone's attention. All you need is to just keep it simple "Be you, and when the time comes be ready to Do You."

That's exactly what Strut did. She gave it her all. She made it her own race for the finish line. She did it by letting her body language and infectious, bubbly personality do the talking for her. There was no doubt she affected the energy in the room on a major scale. It was apparent, that now, people weren't just looking at her costume. They too were revved up by her performance. But more so, it was obvious that they carefully took note of every single move she made.

Dazzle Them

They could see that this little chick had just hatched from her shell, and she was filled with contagious pizzazz. Heck, I believe it was hard for even the most dedicated hater not to like her enticing audition/performance. I'm sure they could see from the look on my face, that I found favor in it too. There was no question after her audition that the game was on; and therefore everyone knew they had to up theirs. If not, there could be one less spot available. In fact, it's obvious that she struck a chord by how they all of sudden took an interest in her when she finished her audition. It was evident they desired to pick her brain a little by all the FATTERING, Oops! I mean flattering comments, and or questions they asked her directly after her dazzling routine. I noticed how they swarmed around her like little bees on honey. And I'm sure some were hoping for just a little drop of her syrupy sweetness to drip off on them.

Hey, if you think kids and their moms and dads who bring them to auditions are not competitive, well then, you better think again. They most definitely are, and they also tend to size up their competitors early on at auditions. Trust me; these parents want to know who's going to be a threat to their little Suzie or Johnny. In fact, it was circumstances like these that made it clear Strut had better watch out. You'd better believe those desperate stage parents/teachers sitting on the sidelines and observing were on high alert. Hey, they were no dummies; they could see that this kid had something special. They knew after Strut's smoking performance, they had no choice but to light a fire underneath their own kid's feet. They knew their child had to deliver nothing less than the goods. Now their mission was to make sure, at all cost, that their kid would be the one to give Strut a run for the money. How could that be? How could one of their little starlets possibly have an edge on Strut, whose dazzling, fiery audition performance had the room on edge? Hmmm! Well, there was maybe one advantage some may have had. And it just might work, if Strut allows it to intimidate her. I'll explain what I mean.

Work, That's What Happens When Desire and Ability Meets Opportunity

Strut's audition was good, but there was one area where she needed work. What was it? It was her technique.

What? Hey, don't get me wrong. Yes, she was superb doing her own routine, but don't forget, it was only part of the audition process. The choreography round was next, and I'm sure her competitors began to wonder if she could go any further. Here's why I say this. You see, Strut wasn't the most technically proficient dancer/performer of the bunch. Her technique was indeed a little weak and she needed more training. I'm sure others auditioning recognized it too, because there were several kids, some of whom I'd worked with before, who had way more technical ability than she did. What does that mean? It means that she couldn't execute things like, for instance, a triple pirouette (turn), or fall into a Chinese split, or do a switch leap, nor could she kick pass her ear like they could. These are all things that most trained dancers, even at a young age, can do. It's safe to say that possibly some of the others auditioning might have thought they automatically had an edge on her because they could execute these things.

Like I said before, some of the kids I had either trained or worked with previously. So they also knew my call back choreography round would pretty much have a few technical elements that would challenge them in one way or the other. They knew as well from working with me, how much I valued and stressed the importance of having good solid training. They knew it would be exactly what they needed to go the full distance. It matched my motto which is to **"Live Your Best by Training Your Best."**

Here's the bottom line. As good as Strut's solo audition routine was, after seeing a few dozen other fabulous routines, many of which were much more technically infused, it was apparent to me that her routine was lacking elements that showed off her technical skills. However, the time had come to make a decision. Let me share with you my thoughts. I liked Strut, but I was a bit concerned about giving her a call back. Why? I questioned that if I did, would she be able to do any of the more technical things? Or would she be able to keep up with the other dancers who were all around more proficient than she might be? I wondered if it were possible to turn this ugly duckling situation, in terms of lack of ability, into a beautiful swan finish. So after thinking about it, this is what I concluded. Although it might be a gamble, I believed it could be a risk worth taking if I gave her a call back. Here's why. I felt that whatever Strut might have been lacking in technical ability, she made up for with raw natural talent. Then it dawned on me: I began to question a few things. I thought, isn't having raw talent an asset? In fact, isn't it true that we all start out with raw natural ability? Isn't it true that nobody begins with having all the elements they need to be at the top of their game? I thought as well, doesn't everybody have to work at gaining those skills? Shouldn't she at least be given the chance to prove that she can do the work?

Cast Me; You'll See

Here's the deal. I'm sure Strut knew her technique was lacking, but she also knew how to work what she did have. It was apparent to me that this little starlet had no fear. Nor did she seem intimidated by all the fierce little competition-trained dancers who gave very technically skilled auditions after hers. I liked how none of this seemed to faze her. Why didn't it? She was living out her dreams and passions. It was amazing and refreshing to see someone move so freely and unrestricted. I really liked how she didn't move so mechanically; like a puppet on a string, which is sometimes what you get from performers who concentrate too much on technique that they can't let loose.

Hey, don't get me wrong. I think it's imperative to get the best training possible no matter what profession it is. Like I said earlier, it is what will give you security and the unwavering ability to be able to deliver the goods. It's your secret weapon. I also think it's equally important to never lose, or restrict, your natural ability. It should always shine through as well. The reason why is that natural ability is something that can't be learned or taught. It's given out at birth. It's embedded in you. It's what makes you unique and sets you apart. We each have something. I know your question to me might be: "but what if you're not sure what it is?" Well, if you don't know, your life's mission will be to keep searching until you find it. Nonetheless, in my book, there was no doubt that for Strut it was being a performer. I thought her freshness, spunkiness, stage presence, drive, and determination brought something new to the table. Sure, she might not be able to plop into a full Chinese split right away. But I believed if she was given the chance to make the callbacks and if asked, she would darn near pull a muscle trying. She would make the effort, and that's exactly what I was looking for.

And I'm glad I did; she didn't prove me wrong by making it through to the call back choreography round with about fifteen other performers. It was there I taught them several challenging routines. I'll be honest; Strut struggled a bit. However, the good thing is, she took my critiques and applied my corrections well. It showed that she was hungry to learn as well as eager to keep up, and to do her best. Did her natural movement ability play a role in it too? It most certainly did. Her natural movement ability worked in her favor, yet it wasn't all she possessed. She also (listen up, here's where smarts, education, and brain power reign) had a sharp eye for picking up steps, good lines, timing, and phrasing. But above all, she knew how to work her facial expressions. As well as she could mimic whatever I did, which is half the battle? How so?

When you're casting for a show, if the person auditioning can't at least mimic well, then casting them might not be a good idea. It's because more than likely they won't be able to keep up. This wasn't the case with Strut; she was a born performer. Her eagerness to give the choreographer what he wanted was good enough for me, so I cast her for the show.

Cross Connect

Next, I was doing a children's television pilot for NBC television back during the late ninety's called *"Hops Spot."* Hops Spot was a show about this really cool secret fantasy place where kids would sneak away to have some private group fun, as well as discuss personal matters. Hops Spot was very similar to the current television show "Glee" where the performers are all pretty much multi-talented, and most are considered triple threats, meaning they can sing, dance, and act. The really groovy part was how the kids arrived to the Hops Spot; they did it by jumping through big round, colorful, circular hoops on the ground that transported them there.

The producers discovered they needed a choreographer, so I was brought in for the show's call back and final casting. Normally, the choreographer is there from the start, but I was game either way. Actually, I thought it was sort of interesting. It was different and rather intriguing to have *no idea* who made the final cut. When I arrived I was so surprised to see that the majority of the kids were kids I'd worked with before. Of course, I was so excited to see them all doing their thing and doing it so well. And you'll never guess, or maybe you will, whom I ran into? Yes, "Strut!" I was especially thrilled to see that she made the final cut. I knew it would be a joy working with her again. When I started teaching the group the choreography, I was amazed at how well she kept up. I was so pleased to see her holding her own. It was a pleasure to have connected with her again. I felt like a proud papa to see her standing strong among this fierce little cream-of-the-crop ensemble!

Groove is Gonna Get Cha!

Years later I was asked to do some choreography for a high school performing arts magnate program. They were doing a musical called**, *"Once On This Island."*** The scene I choreographed took place at a festive location where the islanders went to get their groove on. My job was to create a cool original Afro-Caribbean hip-hop style dance number. I remember how thrilled I was to be doing something unique. In fact, choreographing it was so fun and exciting; I almost cast myself in it! When I arrived to work with the cast, once again, I noticed that there were several kids with whom I had worked before. The really surprising part was I had not seen them in a few years, and I couldn't believe how much they'd grown. It was like a homecoming for me, and I'm sure it was for them as well. Then after our short casual meet and greet, we immediately started rehearsals on the auditorium stage where the show would take place.

Just then it dawned on me - Strut attended that school! I thought, isn't this the troop with whom she often performs? Yet I didn't see her. But I didn't ask why. I just figured she was busy doing other things. However, I thought what a shame! Because I believed she would have enjoyed being a part of such a stimulating cast and groovy routine. Then after several days of rehearsals I finished the routine. The kids loved the dance fusion mix of afro-Caribbean and hip-hop moves. It was so infectious that during one of the rehearsals I was shocked to peek over and see the director, who watched from the wings, getting her groove on too. It was stellar cool.

I believe all the fun and excitement is what provoked her to immediately request an entire run through of the show on stage. She wanted to see how the dance merged into the other scenes. Then as everyone was called into position, I thought it was great and exited the stage. I was so thrilled to finally get the party started, and see how it would all come together.

Rush, Be Seated

So I gladly took to the stairs to sit my little happy behind down and enjoy some dazzling entertainment. Just as I was about to head down the steps in order to sit in the audience, I felt the stage shake like we were having a slight earthquake. Then I looked back and all of a sudden, out of nowhere, a massive herd of girls appeared and were coming right at me. I thought. Holy Mole! I mean they were rushing out from all sections of the stage area like wild horses. It actually looked like a stampede in one of those old fashioned western movies. It shocked the living daylights out of me. I couldn't believe these girls were rushing out from behind the stage like a herd of cattle just to get a seat. I thought, Wow! Come on, don't they know these seats aren't going anywhere? I thought that this must be a really good show, so I'd better quickly get seated, so I can see what all the fuss is about!

Just then the opening scene started, and out came this very handsome male actor. He was traveling in a mad dash going from stage left to right, as he searched for his lady in waiting singing out her name. Then suddenly I was startled again. This time it was by a series of high-pitched screams that nearly made me wet myself! Where were the screams coming from? Get this. They were coming from behind me, and out of the mouths of what looked like every available girl in town. You know! The stampede: that massive herd of girls who had nearly plowed me over. The strange part was I couldn't believe how they decided to sit in back of me. As they proceeded to scream in unison at the top of their lungs, right into my ears. Then I thought, "All this for an actor?" I couldn't believe it. They were acting like he was one of the Backstreet Boys.

That's when I realized it was because of his strikingly handsome looks. Oh, now, I get what all the fuss was about. Yet this shirtless young muscular knight in tight, colorful Caribbean knee high pants didn't allow any of this to deter him. He continued to weave his way through what appeared to be a maze-like set design trying to find his damsel, who appeared to be in distress. Not only was he convincing, but he also had a superb voice that could make even an American Idol finalist feel a little hesitant about having to render a song after him. Then he continued in song and dance to search for his female companion. Nonetheless, it was obvious she heard his voice and began to answer his call in song from far in the distance. There was a barricade blocking the two, and she was hidden behind it, so you couldn't see her. Yet I noticed she too had a beautiful voice that was angelic, and songbird like in nature. As she continued to answer him each time he called with note after note of rich soulful lyrics that expressed her longing, searching, and deep desire for him. This happened all while they both weaved their way through this maze in a crazed search to find each other.

Like I said, only he was visible. The barricade kept the audience in complete suspense, and filled with wonderment, as to who she might be. Then suddenly their voices came together, and she twirled out. Guess who appeared? You guessed it, "Strut." This time she wasn't a chorus girl. She had graduated to become the female lead. I was completely stunned. Though I thought, "it was definitely worth the rush to be seated."

Convict & Convey

Years later I couldn't wait to go see Michael Jackson's "This Is It" documentary movie about his rehearsals for his last London Concert tour. It was pure bliss; I couldn't believe I was finally getting the chance to see the man at work again. It totally "blew me away!" The film was a real package deal experience. It was worth more than its weight in gold and every cent I paid for the ticket just to watch his work ethics, as there was no doubt that he was a professional on all levels. It was evident everything from his brilliant ideas, to his precise singing and incredible dancing ability. It was refreshing to see that the film not only focused on his talents, but it showcased his warm, caring, and passionate side too. I especially found favor in how it depicted his caring nature for people. It was equally such a thrill seeing the whole tour process; everything from the auditions to him selecting the singers and dancers etc. It was funny how I kept looking closer, and closer, at the screen, to see if I recognized anyone. Actually, I did recognize a few familiar faces. There was one person in particular I gave a double take to, until I realized it wasn't whom I thought it was.

Then M. J. started singing one of my favorite songs, "The Way You Make Me Feel". The song is about him trying to capture the attention of a female love interest that, for the moment, seems to be uninterested. Yet he doesn't stop until he eventually wins her over with his persistent charm. The casting was spot on because the girl he chose was dynamite. I mean she hit the stage like a tornado whipping through small towns with attitude, confidence, and conviction. It was like she was conveying to him, "Honey, if you want me, you've got to work a little harder." The girl was beautiful and looked like a statuesque super model. I liked how she so convincingly ignored him, as well as pranced away from him with a powerful diva walk every time he tried to "Put The Make On Her."

Parade, Parade, Parade!

It was totally awesome how she made every hard-hitting stride, and sassy hip sway, fit to the beat and get right to the point. Another amazing thing was how she paraded around like a Victoria's Secret model working and rocking the runway; and all "in six-inch heels." Her womanly mannerisms conveyed and displayed such confidence and strength that if celebs like Tyra Banks, Naomi Campbell, and Beyoncé had been close by watching, they would have considered asking her for a lesson or two.

Then I leaned forward in my seat to get a closer look at the screen as I thought, "This Girl Looks Familiar." I looked once, twice, and then three times, as I nearly fell out of my seat. I think I actually did, I can't remember. But I do remember letting out a scream. Guess who it was? You know it! It was Strut, but this time she was no shy little girl, or developing teenager. She was a young lady, and there was no doubt that she was "All Grown Up!" She was Michael Jackson's female lead. It was stunning to see how she went from portraying Janet Jackson as a little girl, to dancing with Michael Jackson as a grown woman. What a striking transformation!

It was a wonderful day for me as well, as I saw how the bet I placed on her early on paid off big time. The amazing thing was that not only I watched, but so did the rest of the world, this once little duckling turn into a beautiful swan. Afterwards, when I contacted Strut to tell her what an amazing job she did, she was very appreciative. I was so thrilled that she too thanked me for believing in and working with her throughout those tender years. She told me how grateful and amazing it was to see her childhood dream of one day performing with the Jacksons finally come true.

It made me so proud; I too celebrated her marvelous achievement. I knew that one day her persistence, dedication, sacrifice, and hard work would pay off. It's a classic example that shows us that when preparation meets opportunity, "If you work it, it'll lead you to Success."

Here's your "Work + Talent = Results!" Recap @ Work.

(Use These Motivational Groovement Techniques to Help Empower Your Life)

* Never cover up your natural, raw, God given talents or abilities. Let them shine. Use them because they speak volumes and will showcase the real "you."
* Keep it simple and be yourself. There's no need for unnecessary gymnastics or gimmicks if you don't need to use them. Be You & "Do You!"
* Remember talk is cheap, so Let Your Actions Be Your Star Attraction.
* Size up no one, it's not necessary. Know that one size does not fit all. We each have uniqueness abilities.
* Know that everybody can teach you something if you're willing to look, listen, and learn.
* Celebrate your life; get your groove on, even if you have to sneak it in, just like the play director.
* Train your best; and it will equip you with the rest.
* Beware of life's predators who will try to take what's yours. That's when your knowledge/training can be used as power. Let it be the gasoline that fills your tank for life's big race, so that you'll make it over the finish line first, and gain your rightful place.
* Persist; it's the only way to exist. Make your presence known.
* Dedicate yourself to excellence, and it will attach itself to you.
* Believe in the dream you feel inside; keep your eyes focused on the vision you see and watch it manifest itself right before your very eyes! Childhood dreams can become an adult reality.
* Know that an ugly duckling turned beautiful swan scenario can be applied in many ways. For instance,

it's what happens too when you turn a bad situation into one that works in your good favor.

* Don't stop ticking; keep right on a-clicking. It doesn't matter if it's in combat boots, tennis shoes, ruby red slippers, or six-inch heels.

Do
   What's
      Common;
            It'll
         Make You
            Average.
Use Your Uniqueness;
      It'll
         Make
            You
               Exceptional!

Burn The Competition!
(LDG has her eye
on the tiger)

Hold Your Own

This is a story about a little girl of ten or possibly eleven years old at the time. She was a junior company member at the dance company where I resided as artistic director some years ago. I'll call her Little Dancer Girl or LDG for short. LDG was one of the talented soloists who represented the company during competition season; whom I'd choreographed several dance routines for. She was a nice little girl - sharp, bright, and a quick study. But what she really had going for her was the ability to be an outstanding solo dance artist.

Now here's what else I found interesting. She wasn't much of a stand out when she performed group routines for the company. What I mean is she knew how to blend in when it was required. I thought that was great. It proved to me that she had a sense of sportsmanship, excuse me, I mean "sportsgirlship." As she was a team player and it showed. LDG loved to work and collaborate with her peers as much as they admired, respected, and liked working with her.

This duo combination was one reason why she appeared to be more neutral during group routines. I think it was because she felt less pressure and could relax a bit more. Unlike when performing solo routines, where all eyes were on her at every moment. Now, let the truth be told; if you ever saw her perform you'd see why. It's because performing her solo routines on stage is where she really excelled, and came to life. She was like a lit firecracker. Explosive!

There was no doubt LDG was unique in her own way. The reason was she possessed some pretty rare qualities, in which gave her an edge that made her stand out from among other company dancers. Such as: LDG was an extremely hard worker, a good listener, took all her dance classes faithfully and regularly, and even took some additional classes outside her weekly scheduled elsewhere. Obviously it showed that LDG wasn't playing around; she was determined to hold her own.

Adapt No Matter What

She was determined to be her best. What also worked in her favor was her versatility. She could adapt and change dance styles no matter what style she was given. It could be Ballet, Jazz, African, Modern dance, or whatever else. No matter what it was, LDG was always up for the challenge. That is what made her so special. Don't get me wrong though, not every dance style came as easily as slicing a piece of cake. Surely she, like anyone else attempting to do something new or unfamiliar, will certainly encounter challenges. This I think is a good thing; because it keeps us humble. The difference with LDG, unlike many other kids, was I never heard her gripe or complain about a dance style. You would never catch her sobbing about the moves feeling awkward or being too difficult, even if she felt it. LDG just rolled with the punches. She was a real trooper. And if there was a move she didn't understand, or couldn't fully execute, you'd better believe she'd put in the extra time trying to perfect it. She'd find a way to later make it her own.

Another characteristic that worked well for her was she didn't mind getting corrections, or receiving constructive criticism. It was like she lived for it, and it drove her to be her best. This was good, as not all young dancers feel this way.

Many are very sensitive and often don't like to be singled out when given a correction, because it makes them feel like they're being picked on. It was evident that this didn't matter to LDG. Why not? The reason was she was a perfectionist. She was the type that simply wouldn't settle for second best. It's true; she either went the full nine yards or not at all. I think that's great. But what I also know is that being too much of a perfectionist has its down side if not handled correctly.

Yes, it can work against you, if you don't keep it in check. Here's what I mean. Perfectionists want to do everything perfectly and often get frustrated or discouraged when they don't. Does that sound a bit egotistical? I would say, "of course it does." Is it wrong to think that way? Well, I think maybe not; if you can accept that doing your best, whether it's perfect or not is being good enough. Because it is not realistic to think that you can be perfect at everything you do. Absolutely not!

Here's why I say this. Nobody is perfect. Well, no one on this planet! When it comes to people, we all have imperfections. We all make mistakes, which I think is not a bad thing, but rather a good thing. How so? Our mistakes teach us about ourselves. We learn and grow from them. What's good about making a mistake is that it gives you another chance. It provides for you the opportunity to correct the problem. It gives you something to strive for. It's a good thing, but it's not always recognized that way by a perfectionist who doesn't see the value in making a mistake. That's why being too much of a perfectionist may frustrate you if not kept in check. How do you keep it in check? You must be able to allow yourself to make mistakes. They are natural occurrences, and/or tendencies, we each have.

Next, don't be too hard on yourself in feeling like you have to get every move down or perfect right away. The reality is, no one gets everything right super-fast, or all the time. Was LDG an exception? Most definitely not! Remember, all achievable goals take time. Here's another thing. When it comes to learning new or unfamiliar dance moves everyone, yes, I said everyone, including me, struggles at some point. The reason is that not all moves are created equal. The fact is that some moves will come easily, and others will be more of a challenge. Actually, some will even seem frustratingly difficult to master. So don't get discouraged. Know that it's all part of the process, and it can be humbling fun. Remember, the most important thing is to be happy with what you did. Then "let it go." "Know that you did your best, and then give it a rest." Save any unfinished business for another day, or later for your perfect practice session.

What's perfect practice? It's another one of your secret weapons for success. I'll go more into detail about it later. Yet, briefly I can tell you this. It is one of the things that helped LDG with her pursuit to step into greatness. I can tell you this. It wasn't luck like some might have thought. Instead, it had everything to do with LDG's commitment to excellence. I believe if there is such a thing as luck, it stems from hard work and the preparation it takes for being ready to one day meet your golden opportunity. Of course you know, sometimes that means you must be able to adapt under adverse conditions, which is often the true test. It's a test that usually separates the weak from the strong, and for LDG, her moment of truth was about to arrive.

Prep, Position & Perform

Here's what happened next. We were attending a competition and she was in a lineup of about twenty-five or so girls performing solo routines. These weren't your ordinary girls, but like the Miss America pageant, they were all finalists vying to take home the highly coveted first, second, or third place "crowned" position. You'd better believe every single girl there kept close eyes on LDG. They knew from her track record that she was definitely one of the petite threats that could easily be standing in their way.

Here's what was odd. I rarely go backstage during a competition. It's normally my policy to give the performer some space and a chance to peacefully work things out before they perform. This is after we've rehearsed the routine together. However, this time was an exception because for whatever reason I felt LDG needed me. I felt the need to protect my prize possession; the one to whom I knew this opportunity meant so much. Don't forget I too live a performer's lifestyle, so I know how sometimes crazy things can happen during the heated moments of a competition.

I wanted to check to make sure LDG was okay and that she wasn't accidentally locked away in a closet somewhere by an overly jealous, oops! I mean, zealous, pageant girl. Or happened to have slipped and fell on a water spill that some dance mom "accidentally" knocked over while LDG was rehearsing near her daughter. Hey, like I said, this was a competition, so who knows what could happen? I wasn't about to take a chance that something wrong might happen to LDG.

That's why I rushed back stage. And I'm so glad I did. Here's why. When I entered the backstage area the tension was so thick I doubt that you could have cut it with your sharpest kitchen knife. Then I noticed how every girl was intently going over and over her routine while a glaring teacher, dance mom, or dad, watched them with hawk eyes. I mean, they micro managed their every single move; it was like they were putting flour into a sifter to extract even the slightest unwanted particle.

The interesting thing was how some did it peacefully; others did it yelling and screaming. I couldn't believe how they screamed at every wrong move their kid or student made. This, in my opinion, was not the proper behavior to portray in front of the other contestants. Here's why.

I prefer a more sensible and calmer approach (outside the studio) because my groove theory is, either you are ready or you're not. There are only minor critiques and suggestions you can make at such a late date. I believe the cake baking should have been done at the studio and not backstage. What I mean is, either the body of work is complete or it isn't. It's too late to try to do it backstage right before the performance. That's not the time to make the cake but instead spread on the creamy frosting. It is what gives the performer and the performance, the finishing touch. It should be done with words of encouragement that may positively motivate and enhance their performance, and not negative cut downs that may perhaps lessen it.

So backstage I helped LDG clean up and fine-tune her performance in which I worked with her on technique, style, and overall delivery. I personally love working one on one. It gives me pure joy; I like being able to bring out a person's personal best. I find it totally thrilling being able to see the strides and improvements one can make. It's all due to the prep work, because it's about practice and positioning. This is what gives a person the tools they need for a successful outcome. In fact, I enjoy the preparation and process so much that I often need to remind myself not to get carried away.

Deliver The Chills

Well, unfortunately, that is what happened here too. I was unaware that LDG'S placement in the lineup of girls soon to go out was approaching fast - until the stage manager called her. Then I finished up quickly, and exited backstage, so I could get a better view of her performance from the audience. I was actually a little nervous. I thought perhaps, I gave her too much to think about right before going on stage. Even though they were minor details, I feared she might get overwhelmed or confused. Yet then again, I believed she could handle it. And oh boy! Was I ever right about that! What happened next had me in total awe; trust me, that don't happen too often!

I could not believe what I was seeing. In all my nine years of working with the competition team I had seen very few performers like her. Check this out! The minute she walked out on that stage it was like watching a bull being released from the gate at a championship bullfight. It was almost like I actually saw a bull standing there in the ring (on stage) with smoke exuding from its nostrils while kicking up dust. Instead, it was little dancer girl! She was the bull, and she was ready to trample on anything or anybody that got in her way. It was so obvious that she was out to win! Her expressions and dance ability seemed to cry out "I'm a winner!" Here's what else had me so shocked and on the edge of my seat just like the rest of the audience:

I COULD NOT BELIEVE that she executed every single correction I worked with her on! It wasn't that the audience knew, but I could see what a difference it made. Here's another surprising thing: I finally realized why there was always a crowd of girls flooding the backstage area trying to get a peek at her performance. It's due to her performance was picture perfect perfection. It was much like a painter's stroke of his brush creating fine, exquisite, art on a canvas. The difference was she used her body to create one beautiful portrait after another. Her delivery actually gave me chills. Then to top it off, she won the top spot in her age category. She also won the top spot in the overall junior age division, which was composed of about one hundred plus dancers.

Practice, It's Good For You, but Perfect Practice Is Better.

How did she do it? You see "LDG" practiced her routines every day and knew her music inside and out even if by some fluke her nerves kicked in one day and she forgot a move, or lost her way in the music; she could immediately pick it back up without anyone knowing it. Which is what any good performer, or soloist should be able to do. Here's why. There's an old saying that goes, "Practice Makes Perfect." Well, I only agree to a certain point. What you really want is "Perfect Practice" like I mentioned earlier. It's better. Here's why. Practicing only for the sake of doing it can be of little use if you're just going through the motions, and or, practicing whatever you're doing the wrong way. That's why I think "Perfect Practice" is what you should strive for. Why?

It's because if you practice without the goal or purpose being to do it right, then two things could happen. The first thing is you could possibly pick up bad habits, and the second is you will mostly continue to do things the wrong way. This will happen especially if you have doubts about the right way to practice it from the beginning. That's why it's always best to ask the instructor about the right way to execute any given move. If not, then the results will be that your practice will always be heading in the wrong direction instead of the correct direction.

Therefore perfect practice is what will help you to continue to move ahead, and it will also give you an edge. Perfect practice is where skill and talent meet, and when used effectively, it creates mastery. It's the stuff that breeds pro's and it gives them the drive to shoot straight for the top. It's what will help you to achieve being able to be on top of your game. It's what striving to be your best is all about. This is also where those who are perfectionists, (or those who simply have a love and passion for what they do) reign supreme.

Perfect Practice is the only way to go for people like LDG who have a burning desire to be exceptional rather than settling for just being average or mediocre. It's for those who want to avoid not only being on **"The Sit List"** (once again, it's something I will be talking more about in book 2 of the series.) It's also for those who don't want to settle for living their lives thinking they can do this. "fake it till you make it."

Fake It, but Will You Really Make It?

Which I believe is not your best-case scenario. Here's why!

I don't believe, nor am I sold, on the "fake it till you make it" concept. Sure, I understand what some people are saying, that it is better to do something than nothing at all if you're not sure what to do. I would agree, but I think it only works in certain situations. For instance, if you're caught off guard, or are put on the spot with no ability to solve a particular problem, or not knowing how to execute an unfamiliar task. Then yes! You would of course need to perhaps fake, or wing it.

What you might not realize is, even that takes some effort when you're trying to put your best foot forward. Which I'm sure is what you'd hope to be doing, wouldn't you? What I mean is, faking or winging it takes work too. So why not if you're going to do it, make it a successful attempt to learn how to do it right? One of my biggest pet peeves is this: Why should you ever have to fake it if you have the option, and or the opportunity, to learn it the correct way? And there is always a correct way, but it usually takes some work. That's why the "fake it till you make it" concept doesn't always gel with me. Here's another take on it. Let's say you live your life always leaning on the "fake it till you make it" concept, and it's always the route you choose to take.

Tell me, what are you going to do when you meet someone (and sooner or later you will) who isn't faking, or winging it? Someone who knows actually what they're doing on all levels, and they know it from the inside out. Then what will you do? Hmm, I wonder if that concept would have worked for LDG?

I don't think so. Why do I feel this way? Here's why. I don't think if LDG had adapted the "Fake It Till You Make It" concept she would have been so successful. Here's why I say this. That particular competition was actually just the start of many more accomplishments for her. The story ONLY gets better. She went to another event, and burned the competition severely by winning the top overall score out of about 2,000 entries and acts combined. Wow! Now, doesn't that make your hair stand up on your head? I know it did mine! ☺

Here's Your "Leave A Blazing Trail!" Recap @ Work.

(Use These Motivational Groovement Techniques to Help Empower Your Life)

   * **Use Your Talents as They Can Often Take You Far. Just Like Little Dancer Girl.**
   * **Shoot For The Best. Not everyone is meant to be a soloist or can be exceptional at it, but it's in everyone's DNA to give it their best shot at whatever they desire to do.**
   * **Fake It, but Will You Really Make It? The theory "fake it till you make it" may work for amateurs but never for a pro. Don't believe me; just believe Michael Phelps, or Tiger Woods.**
   * **Practice, It's A Good Thing, but Perfect Practice Is Better. Perfect Practice is the best way to go because it builds your confidence and it gives you the assurance that you know exactly what to do, and how to move in the proper way or direction to get there. I know from personal experience that there is no better**

feeling than to be sure of how to properly execute whatever you do or know.

* Win! Win! Win! What Does It Really Mean? Winning is always about doing your best no matter if it's a 1st place or a 3rd place.

Note: Remember: When you step up to meet any challenge; that alone automatically makes you a winner!

* See, what's wrong with C's? We live in a world that highly rewards those who are on their A game, whether it's making a 4.0 honor roll list, or being an A list celebrity. Which is all fine and dandy, but what we often forget is that it takes making a few C's in order to achieve getting on the A list. Well, actually, it's five C's from my point of view. Yes, to be able to set a blazing trail of fire for any competitor coming your way it takes Clarity, Courage, Commitment, Concentration, and Consistency.

Stand
    Realistically
        with
            Raised
                Standards, And
Everything
    Else
        Around
            You
                will
                    Rise!

Make It Hot Like A Jalapeño
Confess It, Serve It Up!

Expect The Unexpected

I had a rather interesting experience once - well, it was more like a life changing experience. I was invited to Monterrey, Mexico where I would be conducting a series of workshops in all styles of dance for a convention. I was so excited to be part of an amazing staff of professional choreographers and instructors visiting from the USA for an extended weekend that I knew would be full of mayhem and fun. We were also judging a dance competition for a very talented group of dance students ages six to eighteen, young adults, and local dance teachers. It was my first time there, so I didn't know exactly what to expect. But I knew the experience would be thrilling because I had heard so much about Mexico; how charismatic and eager the people were -which by the way lived up to its reputation. Let me tell you what made it all so true.

I couldn't believe the minute we arrived at the convention center how we were greeted by a crowd of screaming students, (or fans?). They were acting like we were rock stars! You would have thought they were waiting for someone like the Beatles, Michael Jackson, or Elvis to arrive. I asked myself, "is this a rock concert, or a dance convention?" It was a bit confusing and shocking because the place was jammed packed with wall to wall people who literally jumped like bunny rabbits at the slightest sound of our voices. It totally caught me off guard, as it was sincerely a sight to behold.

What made matters even more interesting was that the congested situation brought with it what seemed like a mob of people. They were desperately waiting as if a rock concert just ended to get a snapshot, autograph, or both, with us. Now here's the strange thing: they didn't mind us writing on whatever they could find. "Like what?" Well, there were standard items, like a piece of paper, a tee -shirt, a shoe lace, or a tennis shoe. Then there were odd requests, like suggesting we sign it on various body parts, such as their wrist, neck, back, or chest. Wait! It didn't stop there. Some made even stranger requests, such as wanting to get a signature written on items like a balled up piece of tissue paper I/we previously had blown our noses on. What! No way! I know what you're thinking! I didn't expect it either!

Crowd Out The Typical

The energy in the room was so electric that it made it difficult for any of us to move a single inch in any direction without experiencing a series of high pitched screams. Screams that were so fierce they would have awakened count Dracula from the dead in bright day light. It was amazing how they seemed to penetrate right through every fiber of our being. Oddly, the place was so out of control that we couldn't walk around the convention center without having to be personally escorted by someone of a higher authority every step of the way. For example, I remember when it was time for us to take our lunch break we had to be secretly escorted away to a private area (more like a hiding place) where we ate quietly, before the mob discovered us. However, when they did, we knew we had to get grooving; it was off to the races in search of another location.

The situation was so crazy; I recall not being able to go to the bath room without someone following me inside to ask for an autograph, or photograph, with them. Sure, it was weird. But actually, I didn't mind. Now here's the funny part, I don't think I've ever autographed so many sheets of toilet paper in all my life. I admit the whole scene was a bit bizarre, especially when someone wanted to take a photograph. Why? It's because the bathroom didn't exactly serve as a very picturesque location. It was no plush Disneyland adventure, having a urinal as a backdrop, but I guess it worked. I'm saying this because it seemed that the mob certainly didn't mind, as they continued to snap away.

Okay, forging ahead, it's the next day and the convention is off and running. It was a non-stop fiesta. The dance competition started that day, Friday, around 3:00 pm and lasted until about 2:00 am Saturday morning. It basically flowed into the first day of dance workshops which were being held Saturday, Sunday and Monday from 8:00 AM to 5:00 PM. Nonetheless it was Friday night, and the center was jam packed with competition routines that seemed to never end. It's usually that way with any dance convention even though most pride themselves with trying to be on time, or even ahead of schedule. It amazes me how the competition always seems to run rather late during the night before workshops. Okay, moving on, it is the first day of workshops, which is always exciting; especially when you get an opportunity like this to instinctively meet such an enthusiastic group of dancer/performers.

Then suddenly we were hit with a big surprise. We weren't told until that day we would be going nine hours, practically nonstop, with strenuous back to back dance classes. The standard amount is about four to five per day. It was quite a challenge, but once again, I was up for it. Well, maybe, until the challenge took a not so typical turn. Here's what happened.

Approach It Naturally

I was teaching a very dramatic slow Latin Jazz routine that seemingly captured the attention of this "wild and spicy" young adult group between the ages of sixteen to twenty something. It was a surreal, but defining moment. After the class it's customary to hug, meet, greet, and shake the student's hands. I did so, as well as enthusiastically complimented them for doing such splendid work. Then I noticed a male student who looked to be about eighteen or so. The weird thing was that he stood in one spot in the back of the room. He stood there staring up at me as though he was in a daze, or in deep thought. It puzzled me, as I couldn't figure out why he stood their staring.

I thought, perhaps I had said something crazy that ticked him off. Now could he be waiting for his golden opportunity to confront me about it? Yikes! Hopefully, it was he was only confused about something? Nonetheless I continued greeting the students; yet I couldn't help but notice him still standing there staring. When the last person left, he immediately approached me. He said, "Hello, my name is José. I said, "Nice to meet you José, my name is Joey." Then I did what was proper; I shook his hand, and complimented him on a job well done.

Don't be Afraid to Ask

He said, "Excuse me, can I ask you a question?" I said, "Sure!" "How do you think I did in your class?" I said, "You did really well." I indeed remembered how talented he was. What I remembered and admired about him most was how technically sound (trained) he was. Not to mention his ability to be able to follow my moves quite comfortably. There was another good selling point I thought worked in his favor, and I'm sure all the girls in the room, or the building would have agreed. It was his handsome looks. As one might say, "he was quite easy on the eyes." Something else: when he danced he exuded masculinity, grace, and strength, which were all fine traits that also had the young ladies heart beat racing. It showed he had a deep passion for dance. Consequently, it was a bit strange, but most delightful, he had all the characteristics that reminded me of myself when I was about his age. (Wink) So, I thought he definitely (in my book) had great potential!

Then he shocked me by asking another question that left me spell bound. He asked, "Joey, please tell me the truth, do you honestly believe a Mexican guy like me could make it as a professional dancer?" I immediately thought, "What does being a Mexican have to do with it?" But I didn't say a word until he finished, as I wanted to give him my best answer. Once again, remembering how talented he was I said, "Yes, you can if you have a deep desire and you are willing to work very hard. He said "thank you" but he slowly walked away with his head down, just as I was stopped by someone else.

Later, after I greeted another group, he suddenly reappeared; once again being unafraid to ask the same question - which really surprised me. I said again, "You are very talented," and told him what qualities he had that stood out to me. Again he said, "thank you" as he slowly walked away and I turned to greet someone else.

Dig Deep

When I turned back around, there he was again; and he repeated the same question. This time he was much more forceful as he surprisingly flung himself to the ground onto his knees and grabbed my hands. As tears began streaming down his face he said, "Do you think a poor worthless brown-skinned immigrant Mexican boy like me can make it in America as a professional dancer. I ask this because no one in my family has ever made it, so how can I? What do I have to offer?"

Wow! His words blew my mind. I was saddened by his statement and shocked to believe that he felt this way. I had never encountered a situation like this before, nor was I sure I knew the right answer to give him. The whole thing caught me completely off guard. It made me pause to think about what I would say. However, I didn't realize it at the time, but it forced me to dig deep and reflect on different scenarios. It made me feel his fear, anger, frustration, and pain over not knowing what realistic future he could achieve. It's because I had once lived through those feelings myself. I too remember feeling like I had no one to confide in about what I was going through.

Choose A Role Model

Having those feelings is what led me to seek a role model. I too was looking for someone I could confide in. That's because successful role models are the examples to be followed by anyone trying to achieve their dreams. In fact, there's no doubt role models are necessary and valuable, especially for boys and young men like José. Having role models early on in one's life is critical. It makes a big difference when deciding which path to take or which person to emulate. This is especially true for those who live in underprivileged areas where successful adult males are scarce. These youth are more susceptible to being led by the wrong influences, and often end up taking the wrong path. It's why they especially need to be surrounded by positive and successful male role models. I'm talking about men whom they resemble and not the ones who grew up with a golden spoon in their mouth. Yeah, I know the term is supposed to be "silver spoon", but I want to upgrade it to "golden" - it's more valuable, don't you think?

What I'm saying is, despite the odds, these men still managed to break the mold and mind set of living a poverty stricken life. I'm talking about men who made a quantum leap into success by fulfilling their dreams and even pursuing a life that's filled with greater achievement, hope, and abundance. How did they do it? They did it by developing traits and characteristics, and matching these to a career that best helped to utilized them. What kind of characteristics am I taking about? They are characteristics such as confidence in themselves, a sense of discipline, dedication, and hard work. And it's no doubt they must be totally committed to doing all the work demanded in order to achieve a successful outcome - all of which is how they turn their dreams into a reality!

That's why it is so important for any up-and-coming crop of gifted boys and young men to have male role models. If only that they can see, and get to know these men who were once just like them. Then they can say, "If they did it, then so can I." They can see how achieving their success shows them what is possible. This is important because they need to know that it's *possible* for them to live a positive, productive, prosperous, and successful life. That's why they need male figures that they can look up to and be encouraged by. It's true that the caring words of wisdom, knowledge, experience, and influence expressed by these men can make a notable life changing difference for them or any other person trying to find their way.

I can truly attest to this, and I'm so glad I had a few male role models in my life. One in particular, Marshall Jacks who was a multitalented African American male performer, choreographer, and dynamic teacher. It was his positive influence that taught me to erase the words, "I can't", and pencil in "I can." I thank him for believing in me when I didn't know if I believed in myself. "Yet it was apparent to me that Jose didn't have this prevailing privilege. I assumed this was due to his limited choices, or not knowing where to find a role model. Not having successful role models is why I believe José saw his skin color as something that would hold him back, rather than propel him forward.

Share Your Worth, but It Begins with Knowing It.

Okay, before I tell you what I said to José, let me say a few things first. Please be patient, this might take a minute. I'll start with saying: I am very grateful and fortunate that I have parents who taught me how to see my brown skin as something that was more of an asset, rather than a defect. I too deeply appreciate them for insisting that I get an education that only confirmed it. This happened when I had the opportunity to study and learn the truth about my ancestors and their history, which was black history. Therefore at an early age I was privy to the truth about what being a brown-skinned person really meant; I knew its true worth. I discovered it to be much more valuable than what I was otherwise influenced to believe by certain surroundings, and some other people. I also learned that my ancestors (who paved the way for me) were hardworking men and women of wisdom, knowledge, skill, wealth, and strength. One of the most important things I learned is they played a very integral part in helping to build, shape, and make America what it is today. Okay - now back to the story!

José's situation, or story, made me think about my life. You see, I grew up in the south as a little black boy having strong hopes, dreams and desires, and one was a strong desire to dance classical ballet. I'll never forget when I went seeking to learn it. My first stop was at a dance academy where the white female owner seemed to be closed-minded. How so? When I walked in and asked about enrolling, she literally looked at me with disgust. Actually, she looked at me like I was trash that blew in from the street. Then she coldly blunted out, "there are no availabilities." But wait! That brush off didn't stop me: instead, it actually fueled my fire.

As I remember I had such a burning desire to learn Ballet that I couldn't conceive of letting anything, or anyone, stop me, so I looked elsewhere. Soon enough I found myself at the door steps of the **Tennessee Ballet Academy** led by none other than the brilliant dance master himself, a white, Jewish man named **"George Latimer."** When I showed up, he made me feel like nothing less than a human being by his kind greeting and sweet words of welcome. Actually, he treated me much like his very own son. I thank him to this day for having arms that were wide open, and a heart as big as the Grand Canyon. I'm so thankful too that when I auditioned for him how he saw my potential, and not the overweight young teenager with low self-esteem. He made me feel alive, important - he made me feel like I *mattered*. This was encouraging to me, and it boosted my self-esteem. I couldn't believe that after the audition, I was granted a full scholarship by him to study at the school! This is what started the process that led me to eventually achieve a bright future. It was one that would years later find me coming back to perform with his professional Tennessee Ballet company and later, with the Joffrey II Ballet.

José's troubling question made me think about another scenario. It was how some of the now famous rappers started out by living in the slums of urban cities. It's true that their lives were nowhere near the picture perfect example of the American dream, either. Instead, their lives reflected a confirmation of the belief that this wasn't America, the land of the free and home of the brave or the America that was supposed to be a place known for its sweet, not sour, "apple pie dreams" and opportunities. In fact, it's hard to believe now, but the reality was, many of those up and coming rap artists could not get a record deal or even have their music played in rotation on the radio like any regular recording artist. So they had no choice but to find another way - a new way - to make their dreams happen.

Yet surprisingly they did. This new way was what became a transition and transformation of self-worth and power, which led them to become the next fresh batch of entrepreneurs who started their own record labels. This turned out to be a blessing in disguise, and a gateway to their many new creative opportunities. This joyous discovery of street smarts and self-worth is what prompted these young moguls to start selling records out of the trunk of their cars. It was a direct way for them to connect and build a fan base that started out with probably a few hundred, then escalated to thousands, and eventually skyrocketed to millions, if not billions of people worldwide.

Outsmart The Competitors!

Later when big shot record executives caught wind of what these young superstars were doing, they wanted in on it and badly. But now it wasn't so easy, because these young cash money crusaders were in a much better position to be able to negotiate more lucrative deals, simply because they didn't need a hand out from these record companies, who, when signing on any new artist to their label usually produced and owned all the rights to their music. In addition to paying them pennies on the dollar for each record sold. Yet, there was one exception: it was different if artists wrote their own songs/raps, etc. It meant they had the opportunity to own the material, and the rights. The good part is many, if not all, of these artists did so. This is what made the playing field a little different for executives who usually had the upper hand. Now the tables were turned.

They realized that they no longer had the upper hand, but had been outsmarted by these clever business men and women. Who were now calling the shots - not in connection with drugs, or bullets, but "money shots," and now the ducks were flying high in their favor. How was this possible? It's because they too knew their true worth.

Slip, but Don't Fall

So thinking about these two scenarios started me thinking. And I thought, surely, if José could see his self-worth as I did, he'd find the value in it. Then my comedic side took over. I thought, "Has this young man (José) gone crazy; does he not realize what gifts he own? Can't he see the god- given talents he's been given? He's a great dancer with a nice slender physique, and has killer looks to match. What the heck could he possibly be worried about? Is he kidding me?" The only reason why this extremely handsome male, who's nothing short of a young Ricky Martin, or maybe even a cut above, could possibly have any fear of not making it as a dancer in America is simply that he might get permanently injured and may never be able to dance again. I know, this sounds crazy huh?

But Wait! Let me explain. This would possibly happen while doing one of his performances. He might slip and fall, permanently dislocating his hip or injuring a ligament when trying to duck and dodge panties and bras being hurled at him by a swarm of screaming girls. Girls who would then try to get their hands on him and rip him apart, limb from limb, like hungry zombies in a horror movie. Get the point? Good! Enough said.

Shine ON!

Okay, now, here's how I responded to José's question. See, I told you it would take a minute, "didn't I?" Well, here's how it went down. I felt compelled to explain to him how I felt about each situation. First, I was rather firm in insisting that he pursue his dance passion, and get going immediately.

Then I let him know that everyone has struggles no matter what country they're from; no one has a free ride. "We all have hardships we must endure. They come to make us prove how badly we want something. But we do have a choice, "we can either continue to fight for it, or we can give in and give up and never get it." I assured him that hardships come with the package in order to make us strong.

Next I made it clear that his brown skin, just like mine, was an asset and not a deficit. It represents strength and power. I also stated that poverty is a state of mind. I explained to him how things don't make you rich. Rather it's your talent, knowledge, and wisdom combined with knowing how to use those gifts to your advantage. I said, "Sure, it might be that none of your relatives made it to, or in America, but their efforts to even try planted a seed that has now sprung up in you, so that now you do have a chance. Know that it's a responsibility to do it not just for you, but in their honor as well. You are the chosen generation. You must go forward so that their work and efforts will not be in vain. Who knows, maybe you're chosen so that their spirit and unfinished work will live on. So you must go forward, and furthermore, I BELIEVE YOU CAN DO IT."

Now here's what happened next. I guess I said the magic words because I saw the tears dry up. Then he said, "Thank You!" However, this time, instead of walking away with a lowered chin, he joyously sprinted away with his head held high. After that incident I stopped wondering why he approached me, as I knew why. It was important to him that I believe he could succeed. Today I know it was my destiny to take that trip to meet José. Now I get why he stood their staring at the stage. Here's the revelation: I saw his shining light through his dance abilities, and he also saw my light through my instruction, and was drawn to it. I believe it was meant for me to meet José to share with him my words of wisdom. What I discovered was in order for my words to really reach him they needed to express strong conviction. They needed to come not from the surface, but rather from the soul. It was a mentor student soul connection. That's the reason why he kept coming back time and time again asking the same question. He knew I could dig deeper. It was almost like he was forcing it out of me. He wasn't about to accept a lukewarm answer. He needed my words to penetrate to his soul; he needed me to **"Confess It, Serve it up; Make It Like A Hot Jalapeno."**

You know, it's like what happens when you bite into a hot jalapeno. It has a sensation that not only burns your tongue and mouth, but it also seems to go through to the rest of your body. What's so surprising about it is, even though it's hot, it's a stimulating kind of hot. It's satisfying. You see, José so desperately needed to hear my words of reassurance, just like I needed to hear them from George Latimer when I was a teen searching for my direction in life. What drew me in was George's shining light, as well as his comforting, and confirming words of wisdom that assured me I had what it took to become a dancer/performer. It made me believe it was imperative that I follow my heart, and pursue my dreams. It was his words that set me on fire, and sent me in hot pursuit of my dreams. Now I realized, I too had the responsibility to gladly pass the torch to Jose that was once given to me.

Here's what that incident taught me. It taught me that each of our lives is important. We are not put here in this big beautiful universe just to live our lives by going through the motions, but rather, we should be about our purpose. That's why it's important to use your talents and continue to let your light shine. Why? It's because doing so is without a doubt an inspiration, plus it will give others who will see your light, and therefore be drawn to it, permission to do the same. Here's a concluding fact. You never know through using your gifts/talents whom you might inspire, or what you could say, that just might change someone's life, **"So Shine On!"**

Here's your **"Hot & Spicy" Recap at Work**

(Use These Motivational Groovement Techniques to Help Empower Your Life)

- <u>Experience Something New</u>, sometimes putting yourself in a new environment just might give you a different kind of experience, challenge, or the boost you need; it could be exactly what you might need to rekindle your spirit.

- <u>Prepare Yourself</u> for life's sometimes unexpected situations. And if it's a good thing, don't resist, it just go with the flow.
- <u>Stand Strong</u> on what you believe in because there may come a time when it might be of valuable use.
- <u>Let Your Voice Be Heard</u>; silence isn't always golden. Especially when you have something that needs to be said that could benefit you or someone else.
- <u>Know Your Worth,</u> as it has a significant value that can either work for you or against you.
- <u>Keep Your Dream Alive</u>. It's important to know that life has its ups and downs and many challenges no matter where you live or what country you're from. These challenges are designed to test each of us to see how much, or little, we really want to achieve our dreams and goals.
- <u>Shine Like A New Penny,</u> or a new pair of shoes. We all have talents, yet what separates the men from the boys, or the ladies from the girls, is those who dare to use them - those who dare to step out from among the crowd and be noticed. It's just like looking at a dull pair of shoes with the realization that the only way you will get them to shine, is to polish them. All it takes is a little effort. Apply a little wax, let it dry, and then rub away. Then set back, relax, and enjoy the work of your hard labor as you see them shine brighter with each stroke.
- <u>Remember The Road Has Already Been Paved For You</u>. Your ancestors made tremendous sacrifices (some it even cost them their lives) just for you to be here. So, if you're reading this, know that completing your journey is necessary and important. It not only leads to your success, but it also honors and continues their legacy as well. Know that quitting or giving up is not an option.
- <u>Don't Be Afraid to Say What It Is You Want From Life</u>, "It's with your mouth confession is made into

salvation." Speak It! And if you're not sure of what you can achieve, don't get discouraged, but do look around you. What you'll find is a big and bountiful universe filled with everything imaginable.

The good book says it's impossible not to succeed in life if you do this. It says, "Ask, and It Shall Be Given to You; Seek, and You Will Find; Knock, and The Door Will Be Opened." Here I will add to this by saying, "When it does, **Step Into Your Greatness!"**

Stop
　　Living
　　　　Your
　　　　　　Life
　　　　　　For
　　　　　　　　Others;
Start
　　Living
　　　　Your
　　　　　　Own!

CALL ME, "DIVA DIANA!"

Pardon Me Please, Queen D Has Arrived

This was an incident I remember far too well. I was doing a celebrity look alike show called American Rock N Roll Soul, in which I worked on the show in several different capacities including being the Choreographer, a co- Producer, as well as a performer.

So one day I was asked by Angie, one of the other co-producer/performers if we could meet. She wanted me to meet her for lunch to see this girl who she thought could possibly be a candidate, and audition her, for the Diana Ross role. I immediately said yes! Actually, I couldn't wait to meet this girl because I knew she must be a stunning beauty, especially for that role. So we met with her at our favorite meeting place, which was a popular old fashion 50's diner style restaurant. And of course when we met, like I imagined, this girl was a total knock out. She had all the physical makings for the part. She was slender, poised, well groomed, and had that flawless Diana Ross glowing skin tone. As well as she seemed to possess elegant beauty queen charm manners too-or so I thought. Until I realized "Queen D" had arrived.

Snap in Z Formation

It all started when we were seated comfortably at our booth and she snapped her fingers asking for the waiter. Yes, she did, really! Angie and I couldn't believe it either. Who is she? Well, I'll call her DD short for Diva Diana. But wait! Keep reading it gets much more interesting. DD began speaking at the waiter, yes! "I said she spoke at him," not to him, as though he was totally illiterate. Then she began describing in full detail what she wanted to eat, and exactly how she wanted it cooked. Yeah, I do remember it did seem a little pushy, but I didn't think too much about it at first. I thought maybe she's just really picky about her food. Which one might think is just a natural thing for a lady who appeared to have such style and grace as she. It didn't dawn on me at the time that her aggressive finger snaps represented something more than just a less than kind gesture.

Rip It to Him Gently

When the waiter returned with her order, the minute he set it down, she immediately ripped into him again. This time it was about how he didn't listen to her specific request as to how she wanted the food prepared. Then she demanded he take it back, which he did. Meanwhile, Angie and I just looked over at each other; only to notice that both of our faces had turned beet red. And that's a little difficult to do considering we're both chocolate bunny, brown skin tone African Americans. Actually I thought, boy! DD is a great actress because she's really working the Diana Diva attitude thing, but isn't she going a little over board? I couldn't figure out why she would rip into such an attentive waiter like she was eating a fresh piece of toast.

Sneak Away Slyly

Yet we remained cool, calm, and collected until the waiter returned. Guess what? Yeah! You guessed it. She had another raging fit about how long it took. However, this time, the looks on both of our faces were stone cold and fully animated. It's funny when I think about it now, but the sheer embarrassment from it all made me visualize the scene from Jim Carey's How the Grinch Stole Christmas movie. It's the scene where the Grinch transforms his hefty potato sack like body into a slinky, slithery snake. He could then slide down the chimney and cruise around on the floor. Instead, I imagined it being Angie and I. We were the ones who shrink into this snake-like image. Then we slid down our seats; underneath our diner booth, and slithered sneaking slyly away. Okay, before I continue, I must let you know what happened before all this. Earlier I wanted to mention that Angie told me there was one particular reason why she wanted me to meet DD before she auditioned for us. Why? It was because she had an unusual personality. Oh! Brother was she ever so right.

Okay, now back to the story. We started the interview and we asked DD why she wanted to be a part of the show. She said, "I need a change; I've always loved theatre and to do this show would be a great way for me to express myself. As well as it gives me a chance to use my talents. Next, we asked her why she wanted to do the Diana Ross role. She replied, "I look up to Diana Ross. I admire her singing, dancing, and acting talents. I like that she's a strong woman who possesses a great deal of charisma and courage just like me." After she said that I thought, okay, maybe this girl was acting after all. Because now she seems so much more relaxed and focused. Maybe I can cancel the feeling of wanting to sneak slyly away.

Fill 'er Up!

Just then DD reached for her water glass which was nearly empty and she immediately shouted out, "Hello, Hello! Excuse me," (the waiter appeared) could you tell me who a person needs to s…. in order to get a refill on water around here?" This time I was at a loss for words. I wanted to do what Carla Flagg speaks about in her story: fold my arms like Barbara Eden did from the classic comedy "I Dream of Jeanne," bob my head, and blink us both to a tropical Island.

We couldn't take it anymore; we were both filled up to the brim. I thought to myself, that's it, there's no possible way for us to continue this interview. This woman had lost her mind. Who did she think she was? However, it didn't end there…

Burst, but Do It with Emotion

After that incident, things took an interesting turn. How so? DD had a reality check. It was like she looked into the mirror and saw that she wasn't the fairest queen of them all. Instead she had turned into the evil witch who desired to get Snow White to take a bite out of the poisoned apple. I think this self-realization is what provoked her to calm down. Honestly, I think she could see that the series of outbursts did nothing in her good favor. She knew it was casting a bad reflection on the type of person she really wanted to represent.

It was making Angie and I feel very uncomfortable. It made her snap to her senses. That's why she suddenly changed like the direction of the wind, and dropped all pretenses. Oddly, she then began to reveal who she really was as well as what she so dearly needed. It was in the heat of this moment DD started explaining to us why she so desperately needed to change her life. Why did she? She stated, "I am not living the life I really want." Instead, she was living her life according to the expectation of how someone else thought she should be. Who was this person? It was her father.

Here's how she described it. DD said, "I grew up with a father who was a very shrewd business man. He lived his life in the corporate world and owned his very own lucrative and prosperous business. He often talked about what a struggle it was for him in the beginning; how he had to work his way up from the ground level to the top. This is how he became a high powered executive. He did this so that I (his only child) could have a better life, rather than the one he had as a kid who lived in abject poverty. He often showered me with gifts. I always had the best of the best, and everything I needed. He taught me to never settle for anything less than what I deserved. According to him, he did this so that I could see if I worked hard enough, I could continue living a luxurious lifestyle."

"I have no doubt some of his mannerisms rubbed off on me, because for years I wanted to be just like him. I mimicked his every move. I followed in his footsteps to become my very own high powered executive, just like him. And on any given day, I worked the corporate board room over, much like a grand prize winning jockey on a race horse. Until one day, I realized something so shocking that it took me for a ride. What was it?"

"It was that the stress of trying to maintain this winning position, or status rather, had taken its toll. Thenceforth, one day it dawned on me that I couldn't live like this anymore. Like what? I simply could no longer live in the footsteps of my father's dream. I thought to myself, who I am I trying to please?" Is it my father, or myself? Whose life is it? Then a little still voice inside of me said, "It was my own." That's when I decided to start living the life I really desired."

Because it became very clear to me that my father's dream for my life was completely different than my own. "Although I loved him dearly, I knew that our lives were not the same. We were two totally different people who wanted, and needed, different things. Unlike him, I don't want to continue living a stuffy lifestyle. For me, I simply couldn't imagine living the rest of my life prancing around in high heels all day and going from meeting to meeting. I want and need to live a life that is freer. I desire to live a life where I can truly let my hair down, and express who I really am. "I want to be a stage performer."

After that DD went on to reveal more of her inner feelings. She said, "I feel like the world is working against me because it doesn't understand me. Sure, I'm a strong woman, but it doesn't make me a snob or a Diva like some people might think. The fact is I really do care about people. I like helping others; making people happy thrills me. That's another reason why I want to be an entertainer." "Here's the thing. I realize what could possibly be holding me back is, I'm an emotional person, who's been letting my emotions run my life for too long. It's time for a change. It's time for it to stop, and I am ready to make that change by taking a step forward." She admitted as well how she thought her beauty could speak for her, and could get her whatever see wanted. But now she realized it could only take her so far.

Wow, I thought this incident was really weird; it made me wonder if she had some sort of emotional instability problem. The reason why I'm saying this is I couldn't quite figure out where this sudden burst of self-realization was coming from. It was puzzling because her entire demeanor changed so dramatically. Nonetheless, it was much more intriguing than what we experienced before. It was a shock to see how this once hard edged tough girl with such a diva infused attitude began to crumble, much like the hot water corn bread we ate as a side dish.

It was noticeable she began to let her guard down, and seemingly volunteered to reveal a more vulnerable side of herself we never knew she had. We were both stunned and I'm sure each had questionable looks on our faces. Looks that questioned such things like, "This couldn't be the same person who took us on a wild roller coaster ride just a few minutes ago?" "Or what happened that she decided to make a hundred and eighty degree turn around?" Either way it appeared to be for the best, as well as it showed an extremely different side of her personality. One that was childlike and girlish in nature. Yet, what stunned us the most was what she said next. Did it lead to another emotional outburst? You better believe it did. This one too was quite different.

Make It A Must

Actually it was rather electrifying. She said, slightly tearful, "I've always had every material thing I've ever wanted. I still feel there is something missing in my life. Although my life has been a good one, I now realize it isn't totally the life I'd hoped for. Instead, it's the one I've settled for. Here's what I mean. I'm not living, or pursuing my dreams, and it has been nudging at me every single day." "I've always dreamed about being a performer on stage; I see it as a means for me to share my talents. Still to this day, I often visualize myself being in front of a live audience. I can just feel the applause, appreciation, and their loving embrace. Unfortunately, I let other aspects of my life get in the way, and I never did what I really wanted to do. I let things stops me. And each passing day the thought of not going for it tears me apart."

"Yet I know why I have not. What's holding me back is fear! I admit it, I am afraid to face my fears. Can you believe a strong woman like me, who can get just about any man she wants, has been living her life in fear?" "Yes, a woman who now realizes that even all the money in the world can't buy me what I desire to have the most. That's the confidence to face and hopefully overcome two of my biggest fears." "One fear is that I wouldn't be good enough to be a stage performer. The other is that a strong gal like me lacked the courage to really try. I realize not doing so has made me resentful and bitter. That's why things must change. I don't want to live my life this way with 'what ifs,' or regrets, by not at least attempting to live my dreams. Therefore I must give it a try, "I must do this audition!" Diva Diana reminded me of Jennifer Beal in the movie "Flash Dance" who also was afraid to face her fears, and therefore took it out on her boyfriend. But he recognized it. He made her see, and accept, her own accountability for not pursuing her dream. Well, what happened? Did DD finally trade in her corporate pumps for a groovy pair of Capezio character heels?

Would she be able to pull off the audition? Could she be the triple threat: singer, dancer, and actress that the role required? Could her strong, aggressive attitude transform, or translate itself into becoming the Diva and mega talent that would blow the other fifteen girls vying for the role away? Would she be able to take over the stage with such commanding presence and force like she did in the corporate boardroom? Could she ace this audition so easily without thinking about it like she often did with sealing the deal on big corporate accounts? Could she have the right stuff? Could Diva Diana be able to sing like a song bird as well as shake a tail feather and rise to the top? Or would she stumble along the way and end up being just another needle in the hay stack?

Okay, here's the deal. DD did audition for the role and she give it her best audition possible. The role required that she be able to perform live vocally, which she couldn't do. Nor were her movements skills strong enough compared to the other girls who auditioned. The bad news is Diva Diana didn't make the show. The good thing is she realized that being a performer was no walk in the park. She saw that it took work;

much like it did to become the high power executive she eventually became. What I admired about DD was, she didn't let the other powerhouse performers she auditioned against intimidate her. Even though auditioning apparently was a new experience and adventure for her, she still gave it her all. I liked how DD never once apologized for what she didn't have or couldn't do. She rather learned from watching how this different kind of profession worked. Then she pulled it together to showcase her best shot at auditioning. Yes! It was a bit over her head but her tough, aggressive demeanor gave her an edge. She exemplified and became the perfect example of how "when the going gets tough, the tough get going!"

That's why after the audition we complimented her for being courageous enough to go for it. Because we knew this audition was a must for her. We could see how she wanted it badly. That's why we encouraged her to start training by taking voice and dance lessons, and after a while possibly audition again. DD seemed excited and I think a bit relieved that she finally did face her fears and went for her dream/ goal. I could tell she appreciated the advice we gave her too. As she later said, "Thank you for the opportunity and encouragement; "Now My New Life Begins."

**Here's Your "Pardon Me Please, As I Take The Step!"
Recap @ Work.**

(Use These Motivational Groovement Techniques to Help Empower Your Life)

Energize Your Attitude

Attitude isn't everything but it's a good start, and it says a great deal about you. A negative attitude can make you appear to be brass, bitter, and bodacious. However, on the other hand, a positive attitude can have the opposite effect. It can give the appearance that you are bright, blissful, and bountiful. So make your attitude one that's positive.

Be Pleasant & Polite

Know that your personality and the energy & vibe you give off can either attract people towards you, or it can turn them away. So make yourself attractive by being pleasant and polite. If you do, people will be attracted to you like bees to honey.

Respect Others and They'll Return The Favor.

You can get a better response from a person when you treat them with respect; such as how you'd like to be treated. **Remember:** It's what you give to the world or universe that determines what you get back in return.

Reveal Your True Self

Good looks (the outer shell) can only take you so far, it can't totally define you. What completes it is when you open your mouth (your insides), as it reveals your true beauty.

Serve Up Some Lemonade

You'll get more with serving people honey than sour lemons. Although, when you combine the two with a little H20 it can certainly make a good batch of refreshing lemonade.

Strive For Success

Success doesn't happen by accident. It takes talent, practice, commitment, consistency, and hard work to get there. Know that there are no short cuts or short roads, it's a long route and ride, but the end results and rewards are definitely worth it.

Develop Your Skills

It's true that any job or career, if you want to be good, or your best at it, requires you to develop the skills you need.

Give It A Try

Never put your dreams on hold or give up on pursuing them without at least giving it a try.

Follow Your Own Steps

Why live in someone else's shoes which could be too big, or too small, or might not fit at all. It is ultimately your own foot prints in the sand that'll lead you to your destiny. Follow your own steps.

Whatever,

Whenever,

However,

Just

START MOVING!

PUT THE NEEDLE ON THE RECORD, SUGAR! "LEAN, MEAN, PLUS SIZE DANCING MACHINE"

The Carla Flagg Story (in her own words)

DO YOUR THING AT ANY SIZE!

From a young age and even to this day, I've always liked to watch folks dance. My favorite dance movies are "West Side Story," "The Red Shoes," "Dirty Dancing," "Save the Last Dance," and of course, "Flash Dance." Can't you just hear the song now, "She's a maniac, maniac on the floor and she's dancing like she's never danced before." I can remember being in high school, wanting to rip my sweatshirt for that cute off the shoulder look from the movie (but never would, because my mother would be upset if I ruined good clothes), locking myself in my bedroom, blaring the music and trying to dance like Jennifer Beal from the movie. I guess you can say I am a "closet dancer" and would find some tranquility and peace for my soul in the motion and music of dance. Some people find their sanctuary in the church or walking along the beach or sitting in the park, but imagine if you will a sanctuary of movement that can be found in a room with hardwood floors, mirrors on the walls, and a stereo system, which is fondly known as the dance studio.

But before I get started, let me introduce myself. My name is Carla Flagg, a 37-year-old architect, 5'-8," 254 pounds, voluptuous, African American female from Pasadena, California. Now, you're probably wondering about the title "Lean, Mean, Plus Size Dancing Machine" and how those elements go together. Well, let me explain.

Lean – Meaning, a size 0-3 will never be me, but I'll take a firmer, smaller, Carla, who is the true girl I see.

Mean – I am strong and confident. I can accomplish anything, if I put my mind to it.

Plus-Size – That's where I am right now, figuratively speaking. <smile>

Dancing Machine - Well honey, that's how my Choreographer/ Dance Instructor (Joey L. Dowdy) best describes me because I love to get my Groove On!

If you talk with my mother, she would say "I love my baby and she looks just fine." My husband would say, "My wife has beautiful curves and is sexy to me". My doctor, well, he has a different point of view. A few years ago he would say "you are morbidly obese, have high blood pressure, and really must lose weight to be healthy." But now he says, "Great! You're losing weight, Keep up the good work." I thanked him for those encouraging words, but who was I kidding, I knew I wasn't totally ready or committed to being a Girl on the Groove. Why? It's because I can do better. You see, I too have been one of those folks stuck in the zone of losing and gaining the same 30 lbs over and over again, until now I am finally totally committed to ending this cycle.

Fog! Fog! Go Away!

Here's my story. All my life, starting from childhood, my weight issues covered me as in a thick fog that would keep me invisible. This "fog" kept me closed off from the world, from my emotions, and would attempt to keep me from achieving my full potential in life, because at times, I would not even try a new activity or event because of my weight. It created for me issues.

Issue #1 I use food as my comforter even when I'm not hungry to cover up my pain and frustration.

It was almost like a scene from the horror movie. "The FOG" where there were these creepy, crawly things (my issues) attaching themselves to my body one by one and slowly engulfing and molding me into a shield of false protection. I called this my "fat suit." I fooled myself into thinking that this "shield" was a test or barrier to find true friendship, by making people think that with me everything was cool and that I had my life in control. Honestly, I knew I didn't. But I thought it would make them want to be my friend, or just like me.

Issue #2 I trust the validation of others before my own.

On a daily basis, I would wear my public image like a mask and I got very good at hiding the real me under layers and layers of pain and unresolved issues. I lived for many years with the self-image and safe identity of "Carla Flagg, the heavy set girl with the pretty face and smile," I now realize that it was good to have at least a "pretty face and smile" because they are my distinguishing characteristics that attract people to my personality; it's still a bit uncomfortable for me, but I am learning to accept and embrace it. But, while living in the "fog," I was struggling inside that unhealthy "fat suit" by pretending I felt great, when I knew my unhealthy lifestyle was slowly leading me down the wrong path and a road paved with all the wrong intentions, such as high blood pressure, the threat of stroke, or a heart attack. All of which would have sooner or later led to the #1 killer of women in America, "Heart Disease."

I knew Deep down inside I really wanted to be healthy and thinner, but for many years I didn't have a clear vision or a plan on how to achieve it. So I tried dieting, and for me it was just about every diet in the book, along with diet pills, liquids fasts, weird food combinations; anything I thought would get the weight off quickly. But guess what? None of it worked. I realize now they were only temporary quick fixes that usually ended with me doing the same old song and dance: gaining all the weight back, plus some which would leave me to feel angry and depressed. Sound familiar, anyone? I as well began to focus all my attention on my body image and what number I was on the scale. Now I know these things were totally the wrong approach. Plus they totally exhausting me so much that it made me want to perform a magic trick, like "I dream of Jeanie" where I fold my arms, nod my head, and wish/ blink myself thin. That's funny huh? What's even funnier is thinking that you could wish yourself thin, which is not the answer, nor did it work. However, it made me realize one thing, "that I needed to stop torturing myself "(mentally and physically) over this weight thing. So, I decided it was time to improve my game by not doing the same old song and dance I call "the lose it, gain it back blues," by adopting a fresh new jazzier tune/approach entitled "Go! Weight Releaser Go!"

This time I'm properly putting the action behind my "wishes" and so far in doing it I have discovered it's not as complicated as I imagined. Read On!

Issue #3 I don't always get the love and support from my family and friends that I need.

Weight Releaser, Baby! ™
(Checking in My Luggage)

Say it Strong, say it Loud, "I am a Weight Releaser, Baby." That's my new mantra. One lesson I've learned is that when I finally commit to a "Weight Releasing" Program, that proper nutrition (which means for me and my household no more fast food stops, drinking more Arrowhead, or Avian water, we're going green and all natural) is essential. The next step is what I call "releaser action." It's something I so desperately need. This action is called "Exercise." Exercise is indeed the key that unlocks the door to a new beginning. It'll help you to release and let go of the unwanted stress, toxins, and pounds.

That's why I like being a "Weight Releaser", which is what I prefer to call this journey to healthy living, because from my past experiences I don't like using the word "diet." Think about it! Why focus on a word that has "die" in it, when you should be focusing on "living" your life to its fullest? Hey Now, Strike A Pose! The word "Weight Releaser" has a better ring to it anyway; it just sounds like victory. Besides, being a "Weight Releaser" means that I'm finally identifying and letting go of the physical and emotional baggage that I've been carrying for years or as I call it, "Checking in My Luggage." In return, I will accept a ticket to receive the fulfilled life I deserve. And the first few steps to my fulfilled life starts with me learning to love and accept myself just the way I am. This means I will no longer mentally beat myself up, because how can I expect others to see or love me, if I cannot even see or love myself? It made me think had the "fog" become so thick, that I could not even see *me* anymore? I have to admit, that thought scared me for a brief moment, but not for long because I was convinced there would be no more back peddling. I had to accept that where I am right here, right now, is the perfect starting point and from now on its full speed ahead.

I knew there had to be a better way to getting healthy and fit. Yet it required me to step out of my comfort zone; that's when I made the connection. This is "A Lifestyle Change." It's a daily regime that combines exercise, good nutrition and a positive mind set. It's a process in which my husband and I will do together. We will motivate each other daily to be healthy and fit. Another thing is I found these elements to be the missing puzzle pieces that I couldn't quite put together in the past. I realize they all work together to produce a complete picture. In years past, I would try to exercise without having good nutrition or a positive mindset (wishing myself thin) or focusing on nutrition without exercise. Like I mentioned earlier it was time to start checking in my luggage.

(Luggage Check #1 – Stop looking for the quick fix and focus on the right "Weight Releasing puzzle" that works for me and my body!)

Then after I read one of Joey's inspiring quotes entitled, " Say Away with Depression and Hello to Progression" I realized that feeling crazy, drained, and out of control were merely symptoms that I had lost my groove (Motivation, Stamina, and Control) now it was time for me to Get My Groove Back. (WATCH OUT STELLA!)

(Luggage Check #2 – Self-love comes from within, so I am learning to see, accept, and love myself all over again)

I am no longer living a fantasy life of "wishing" myself thin but I truly realize that actions and efforts are the only way to see progress. This new life style inspired me to search for the next piece of my weight-releasing puzzle that included finding a physical activity I enjoyed. So I took my first step (people told me I moved well) in the right direction of movement: I started taking "Dance lessons." I couldn't believe it, but the piece fit, it was a perfect match. Yes! It was/is exactly what I was looking for. It was something exciting, challenging, and hardly boring, which kept me coming back for more. Right away dance class gave me the rejuvenation I needed, my spark of motivation returned, and it came with a positive feeling that I had indeed accomplished something.

(Luggage Check #3 – Find a passion for movement that will help you find your groove! Look for something motivating that gives you a zest for life.)

I loved everything about dance class including the warm up, the stretching, and the choreography. Oh boy! The choreography part really made me put on my thinking cap, it was great brain food. Wow! I thought to myself this doesn't feel like exercise(the word "exercise" can be a bit scary for some plus-size divas), it's way too much fun, and I'm able to freely express myself through the movement, yet I'm working up a fierce sweat. What more could a girl have asked for? It felt so surreal. Plus, child, I was using muscles I never knew I had. Oh what a feeling! The experience for me was truly the beginning of my new transformation.

The Fear Factor!

Don't let fear stop you from trying something new.

Okay! As I mentioned earlier the word "exercise" can be a bit scary for some "plus-size divas." Here's why. At my highest weight of 294 pounds, I remember thinking like most plus-sizes I had to be smaller in size in order to do certain activities such as dancing, going to the gym, lifting weights, swimming, aerobics, etc. Well, I've learned it's a big misconception and you can do them all at any size, just remember to start slowly and work your way up. I'm fortunate to have discovered dance and I am grateful that I did not let the "fog issue of fear" stop me. I encourage anyone who wants to change their life to find one activity and start today, right now; moving/grooving at whatever size you may be, just find something fun that interests you and start doing your thing. I believe that if you don't find your passion for exercise or movement, then it will feel like a chore and as we all know chores can be easily discarded and placed on the backburner.

(Luggage Check #4 – Don't let fear of the unknown or fear because of your size stop you from trying something new.

Once I found DANCE, an activity that I truly enjoy, I realized that this was something I could do for me, and it only took a little effort. Plus, it was a natural stimulant (not a quick fix) and every time I did it, I instantly felt better about myself. And the other added bonus was, slowly but surely, I was experiencing the benefits of Cardio Activity of dance and fitness which I later learned from Joey was far greater than I ever imagined. Check this out!

Listed below are Joey L. Dowdy's **Groove 2 Improve Fitness** tips on the benefits of Cardio Fitness and Why Dance is Effective.

*Full Cardio!
What you may not know:

❖ Cardio provides oxygen and circulation to your lungs and heart.
❖ It gives you better-controlled breathing patterns.
❖ It detoxifies your body.
❖ It helps reduce memory loss.
❖ It builds stamina through repetitive movement.
❖ It relieves stress.
❖ It burns fat.

8 Reasons Why Dance is Effective!

1. It increases your Range of Motion and Flexibility!
   ❖ Stretching * Balance * Elongating Moves
2. It Boosts Your Self Esteem!
   ❖ Better Posture * Better Concentration * Better Focus / Awareness
3. Builds Stamina & Rejuvenates Your Spirit!
   ❖ Cardio repetition *Deep Breathing * Decreases Stress
4. It Improves Your Coordination!
   ❖ Through simple & complex movement combinations.
5. It Detoxifies Your Body & Builds Stamina!
   ❖ Burns Calories * Cleanses your Pores * Releases Toxins
6. It's the Original Body Language!
   Communication through Movement
   ❖ Freedom of Expression <joy, sadness, love, etc>
   ❖ Situational Workouts <for tough days>
7. It Builds Superior Strength
   Through Therapeutic Healing Exercises
   ❖ Body Alignment * Core Conditioning* Builds Muscle & Produces Strong Bones

8. It Makes You Smile
   It's a simple but effective exercise that always leaves you feeling better.

Discover it! That's what happened when I Found My Dance Passion

[At this point in my life, any kind of movement was better than nothing at all, and I was doing my best to keep up and end on the beat like everyone else.]

My passion for DANCE first began when I stepped foot into a dance studio **(Athletic Garage)** in Hollywood/Pasadena, California to take classes with "Fire Ball" Choreographer/Instructor **Joey L. Dowdy, AKA Dr. Dancer,** the creator of **World Dance Groove™ & Groove is Gonna Get Cha!™** whose endless energy and thought provoking choreography makes you step outside the box. His movement seems like metaphors for life. Why? Because Joey always says, "You've got to find your expression through the moves: you can't be stone faced and just do the steps. Oh! Honey No, he instructs you to feel the moves: you must emote with passion, as he says "dance is body language." You use your entire body to speak and tell a story (creating a beginning, middle, and an ending): "Your Story." Just like life, I existed for many years behind a mask (my stone face) just doing the steps, but once the weight issues are released, you begin to realize that life should be "lived to the fullest" and not just a simple dull existence.

He instructs the class in all forms of dance which include everything from Jazz, Ballet, Afro-Latino, and Contemporary to Middle Eastern, Hip-Hop, and more. He also puts on theatrical dance productions for Stage, Television, Dance and Fitness expos that are rather refreshing and unique. He truly is "Mr. Movement with a Message." I am so proud to say that I feel quite fortunate that I've been able to use my skills and talents in a few of his projects/shows, where he considered and created fabulous roles for big girls like me. Hey! She's a

Maniac, Maniac, and she's dancing like she never danced before. Yeah, I found my passion!

Set The Stage, My First DANCE Class

Okay, so I need to set the stage regarding my first dance class. I walked into the dance studio and moved straight to the back of the classroom, because remember, at that time I functioned in a cloud of invisibility. I mean I was looking for a spot where I felt the most comfortable, had a good view of the instructor and of course, no one behind me. Once the music began and the movement started, it seemed as if the rest of the class disappeared. I immediately transformed and got into the groove. I felt free to express myself and move. I didn't even see the "skinny girls" that surrounded me, because finally I found a passion for movement that I solely enjoyed. What I liked is, it was definitely something I could do for me. I felt so enthralled to be able to imitate Joey's every move. Like I said earlier, at this point in my life any kind of movement was better than doing nothing at all. Honey, I did my best to keep up and end on the beat like everyone else. Believe me! It was no small task (Smile); let me tell you, this sister had to work to keep up!

What I appreciated the most about Joey was that from the first day of taking his dance class, he never once saw my size as an issue; in fact, he embraced it. He said, "Girl you move like the wind, like a dancing machine." I was shocked and I thought "no way," I'm not small and petite (like some of these other ho's up in here – and please imagine this voice in my best Monique (the comedian impersonation). I remember thinking, "doesn't he see I have a few extra curves and a little meat on my bones?" Let's get real! But my size didn't really matter to him, because Joey truly believes, "that dance is a gift sent from up above and it is meant to be shared with everyone."

Issue Releaser: Hearing these words of encouragement was like a ray of sunshine breaking through the issues of "fog," like it was being lifted.)

From that point on, I was hooked. I love how Joey works his entire class; I mean I seriously sweat bullets. His classes are challenging, yet so much fun as well, and it doesn't matter if you are a size 3 or 33, Joey's motto is "You've got to Groove 2 Improve! Now give me one more set, please. Every class I look forward to something new and Joey cuts me no breaks due to my size, either, which is what I need. I mean, his classes are very beginner friendly; he allows and encourages each person to execute the dance movement according to his or her level of ability.

Physical Releaser: Through dance, I have greater cardio endurance, range of motion, flexibility and strength. The choreography challenges me both mentally and physically and is a full Body, Mind, and Spirit experience) Now that I am beginning to advance Joey has me kicking, leaping, and attempting multiple turns just like everyone else. And man, do I love it! I may not always get it on the first few tries, but I don't give up. I keep trying. Because for once in my life I feel that I am not judged because of my size (I feel free and inspired to attempt new movement; it makes me work harder) and it actually feels good to get equal treatment. Why? I am tired of others placing limitations on me because of my size and more importantly I am tired of placing limitations on myself. By getting equal treatment in dance it allows me to reach beyond my limitations, and by understanding how my body works, it has opened doors to other areas of possibilities and capabilities in my life.

Each class offers a different reward, a different chance, and an opportunity to reach higher. I've learned some valuable lessons through dance; useful things that I'm adapting to my everyday life. Such as it's helping me get in shape, stay on track, and it's keeping me in check as I take this journey to the ultimate me. Here's what else I've learned.

Start but Do Finish

1. In dance, it is necessary to not only start the routine, but finish the routine as well. Joey says all movement has a beginning, middle and an ending, as do our lives. In dance there are two essential elements: getting a good start and getting a good finish. Why? A good start teaches you how to

trust your own judgment whether you're right or wrong. It's the true test in knowing that you have the ability to execute the moves on count, and then be able to head in the right direction. It gives you reassurance because sometimes as you're learning and growing you will get lost in the middle. The key is to keep going, stay encouraged, focused; and pick it back up when you can. The thing to remember is to never lose sight and make sure you follow through on the next important element, which is a good finish/ending. The ending teaches you the importance of completing what you've learned. Therefore what that gives you in return is the feeling of accomplishment. Both processes are equally important.

Take Care of Me

However, I have to admit that something else was happening during my moments of sanctuary that I now call "dance class." I began to realize how it was also helping me tackle some of the issues that have been plaguing my weight loss success for years.

Listed below are four ways it has helped me. It taught me to:

1. **Make time** for myself and stop putting everyone's needs before my own.

2. **Let Go of Stress**
   The dance studio is an alternative place for me to release the daily stress from my busy job. It has also become a physical activity that supplies my need for a healthy sense of comfort during stressful times, rather than relying on food.

3. **Trust Myself**
   It's empowering me to be confident in trusting myself and my movement capabilities.

4. **Connect in More Positive Ways**

Dance class provides a wonderful, friendly, and safe environment that allows me the chance to connect with others of like-minded interest who also give me the support and encouragement I need to come out of my shell. Now when I go there, I'm so much more confident and it's no more hiding in or behind the "fog banks".

Being a "Girl on the Groove" has opened so many doors, that I sometimes need to pinch myself to believe.

In the early months of **2005,** I was shocked when Joey asked me to be in his DVD series called **"Joey's World Dance Groove Cardio Dance & Exotic Tone and Stretch".** I said, "Sure, what do you want me to do, help build your set?" (he knew I was an architect) When Joey said, "No, I want you to dance" I have to admit, I was proud to realize how far I'd come. I relished this golden opportunity to represent plus-size women, and hopefully I will inspire them or perhaps even you to find your fitness passion. Then it dawned on me after I finished filming the video how handy the DVD would be when I'm away on business trips. I thought, "Finally I've found a fun way to work out and a video that represented people of color and all shapes and sizes." "I WAS ON CLOUD NINE until tragedy struck, which set me back a bit."

In November **2005**, I was a in a car accident, which destroyed my car and I spent many months during **2006** being treated for lower back and shoulder injuries. The entire experience made me realize that life is a precious gift that should not be taken for granted and whatever issues were still holding me back from living a fulfilled life needed to be addressed and tackled. So in **2007,** I was selected to participate in **"Groove is Gonna Get Cha!"** One of Joey's programs filmed in Los Angeles for ABC News ("Healthy Living" with Denise Dador). It was a year-long campaign with me and another student, Laura Lee, where the focus was on New Year's Resolutions for people who wanted to lose weight in 2007. It was a great success, and for me a new discovery! It helped me to find the pieces to my weight releasing puzzle.

The even better news is now that the program is over; I am "Fired Up" more than ever. I am continuing to work with Joey L. Dowdy who is coaching me every step of the way. He has an exciting program where each week I'm charting my Progress! Success! It has been a wonderful opportunity to finally tackle my issues with weight and start "living" again. Now, I can finally feel myself getting back in the Groove! During this journey, I can share how I've lost 44 pounds and gone from a size 22/24 to a size 16/18 and have lost inches over my entire body, and I am still a work in progress! Sure, I know there are some people who will question shouldn't the weight drop be more? However, what they may not realize is, for me, the weight lose regardless the number is a huge feat. I have not been this size since college, and it feels great. I believe the most important aspect of this journey was finding myself again and being happy. I have not just a physical but a mental strength, and peace of mind, that inspires me to be better; to continue on this journey. The weight releasing puzzle pieces no longer frustrate me, but inspire me to be better. I read once that all great success stories start with a vision and motivation.

Well, DANCE does that for me by keeping me inspired and one day soon you too will witness my ultimate success story! The headlines will say, "Watch out for Carla Flagg, **"Lean, Mean, Dancing Machine."** Did you notice I left out the plus-size? Child! Don't get me wrong, I can still do what I need to do as a PLUS-SIZE STARLET. The difference is I am now claiming a new me, and the new complete me comes with a refined hourglass figure. Hallelujah! It is nice to be a "Girl on the Groove!" because baby, the steps on this journey just keep getting better and there is no stopping me now!

Hard
  Work
        Is
        Heart Work
If
  You
   Do
     What You Love!

Shimmy Like the Rent is Due! (Pay in Sweat) Meet Funky Mr. T

Fly Butterflies

I was so thrilled to finally get the opportunity to take a summer visit out of town. Well, actually, I was auditioning for a performing arts college that I had heard so much about. I was excited about taking this trip that the very thought of it gave me butterflies. That's because I worked so hard saving up my precious dollars for a special trip I knew would mean the world to me.

Fit In Where You Can Get In!

I was ecstatic, as I knew it would bring about new life and excitement. I had my heart set on it being a different kind of experience - one that would be worth every coin I spent because, as I mentioned earlier, I had heard so much about this fabulous school in Pittsburgh called "Point Park University (PPU)" that had a reputation for its brilliancy in the performing arts. It was such a thrilling feeling that I simply couldn't delay the trip any longer. I know - it all sounds so "flash dance," doesn't it? I was so moved because a friend told me how exceptional their dance and theatre program was. He said they had a jazz dance program where the dancers were so outstanding that they performed jazz as exquisitely as the New York City did ballet. Wow! How superb, I thought. In fact, I didn't know such a thing was possible. I had never heard of it before. I was so amazed that I couldn't believe what he was telling me. I thought, I must go and experience this for myself. At the time I was on scholarship at the Joffrey II Ballet, so all I was studying at the time was pretty much ballet. Don't get me wrong, I absolutely loved the Ballet training, and all the amazing teachers I had. I loved the fact that ballet was challenging, yet it gave me the technique, style, grace, rhythm, and artistic development I needed.

However, I felt I needed more versatility. I guess it was due to me growing up as a kid in the theatre world and being exposed to different dance styles. Plus, theatre allowed me the opportunity to use my acting and singing talents as well. I believed not being able to do these things is what had a big impact on why I was feeling this way. You see, I always envisioned myself as a versatile male dancer who could do it all.

I was heavily influenced by the mix of qualities I saw in male performers. These were men like Baryshnikov (famous ballet dancer), Arthur Mitchell (the first black male dancer with New City Ballet), Ben Vereen (Broadway Star), Gregory Hines (Tap Dance & Actor Phenomenon), and to top it all off, Mr. Gene Kelly, one of Hollywood's most beloved triple threats, who was able to do it all. He sang, danced and acted. Doing all three art forms was the vision I carried around in my head. So to me, achieving this vision would only be possible if I branched out and tried a different school with a more versatile curriculum. I figured this would be what I needed to reach my goals. And from what I had heard, Point Park University was the place that had it all under one roof. It was why I so desperately needed to audition for this school. I just knew it would be the perfect fit for me, and in addition to that, make a long-awaited dream come true!

Audition is My Mission

Well, the day finally arrived. I couldn't believe I was standing on the campus of this legendary institute. The fact that it was a blistering hot summer day did not dampen my excitement over auditioning for PPU'S fall enrollment. Before I and twenty five other students began the audition, it was explained to us that not all of the regular teachers were available. Some teachers were on summer hiatus. Therefore, the audition process would be shorter than normal. There would only be two audition classes for the evaluation. Which I thought was fine with me. Sure, it would have been a joy and a wonderful opportunity to meet the entire teaching staff and to learn from them - which I was looking forward to doing. However, I was just so thrilled to be there, that taking even half a class would have sufficed. I was simply loving and living the experience, the city, the people, and the whole process. And speaking of the audition process, I bet you're curious to know more about it, aren't you?

Okay, here it goes. As I said earlier it consisted of two classes, one class we knew for sure would be a ballet class, but we couldn't quite figure out what the other class might be. A wild guess would be a modern dance class. Why? Well, because it's normally what most schools give as a contrast to a ballet class. Plus, modern dance was, like ballet at the time, one of few dance styles in which you could major. Meanwhile, the suspense was building as we sat on what felt like pins and needles of intrigue, wondering what the second class might be. Just then they announced it would be a jazz class. Then suddenly every bun head in the room applauded with excitement, because they knew it would be something special. It would be what we needed: something challenging, exciting and fun.

So, up first was the ballet class. It was given by a very knowledgeable and gifted female instructor. Her moves were challenging, but also fluid, and as smooth as silk. She was definitely an inspiration and highlight all by herself. It gave merit to the school's great quality and the ballet class evaluation that was being judged by a panel of experts who seemed very passionate about their work - although the looks on their faces varied and were a bit frightening at times. Wow, I admit, this really does sound so "flash dance." Another thing: we were told this audition would be considered placement classes for determining what level we would be going into if we were selected. So after the ballet audition which was given in studio one, we were instructed to head on over to studio seven for the second class. This would be the jazz class audition given by "Mr. T." Well, that's what I'm calling him for this story.

Before I go on, here's some more important information. Point Park University was an old hotel building with multiple floors which had been refurbished and turned into class rooms as well as fully furnished living quarters. This was all made possible for students who wanted to pursue a liberal, and/or fine arts education. In addition, this well-equipped building included elevators that would take you to any floor or destination. This means it was able to take you directly to all seven dance studios, except for one - Studio Seven. It only took you part of the way, and then you had to resort to another form of transportation. Can you guess what it was? Did I hear you say stairs? Yes, it was using your festive feet to take the stairs. So it was "up, up, and away we go" on to what felt like a magical journey up the yellow brick road to Studio Seven. Now what I didn't mention is that it seemed like a hidden place where people who only had special permission could go. So we continued onward, climbing the steps to a land that appeared to be like dance heaven. What confirmed we were heading in the right direction was the allure of this cool, funky techno bass music blasting away. It was coming from what appeared to be the hallway of the future. Which meant there was no doubt we were heading in the right direction. It was so stellar, and each pulsating beat blasting from those speakers made the anticipation of our excitement grow even stronger.

Actually, it made me think about the magical scene from the Wizard of Oz where you couldn't see the wizard behind the curtain, but you could hear his voice. Except that this was a door we were climbing towards, and who was behind it - this too was a mystery! There's no doubt in my mind that this audition was definitely a mission well worth waiting for. Boy, the thrill of it and of every coordinated step (to the beat of course) we took seemed almost like we were doing 'chasses' (a dance move meaning "to chase") through the Emerald Forest in hopes of finally getting to see the man behind the door!

Meet A Mentor

Then finally we reached the top, flung open the door, and like magic, the wizard appeared. Who was he?

He was this `5 7` bleached blond Caucasian man with a strong build who wore wire-rimmed glasses and had a neatly trimmed mustache. And boy, I could tell right away Mr. T. took his craft seriously as he even dressed the part. Well actually, now I know, it was more like his version of dressing for success. What also caught my attention was that even though he was teaching a dance class, not one single strand of hair on his head seemed to be out of place. But here's what really had me puzzled. I couldn't quite figure out why only the sides of his hair were wet, especially with all the sweating he did. It was a mystery that didn't reveal itself, "Until..." Well, a little later on during this journey.

Okay, now, more about his dress. He wore a very creative clothing ensemble. Actually, it was one of the most interesting ensembles I'd ever seen. He had on a nice scoop neck tan top t-shirt and red tight fitting spandex jazz pants. It was interesting how he tucked his pants legs into a fierce pair of red stretch leather bitching jazz boots, accompanied by matching leg warmers over the top of them. He also wore two bandanas, both of which he folded and twisted into a string. Then he tied one around his neck, and the other around his leg warmer near to his ankle. Which I thought was not only unique, but just too cool!

Honestly, I had never seen anything like it. By looks alone this new mentor experience had me floored. Here's the most astounding part: even though this was only a dance class you would have thought it was a night club, or disco. Why?

It was because the music was pumping and the dancers were certainly thumping. The only thing missing was the disco ball and the flashing lights, but certainly his attire had that covered! Okay, here's more about the dance audition.

Stand Out And Stand Apart

Starting off, Mr. T. took us through his regular stylized dance warm up, which he derived from a famous New York choreographer/Instructor named, "Luigi." Then he broke into one of his really neat funky jazz routines choreographed to one of the hottest current tunes at the time, that set us students and the dance floor ablaze. I was so in awe because I had never seen a white dude who was like a funk machine. Mr. T. hit all the right accents in the music plus he knew how to fuse his stylized dance steps in with several current social dance steps that made young fries like us swoon with excitement. I felt like I was dreaming, and at any minute I would awake up from this incredible experience of living in a Techno Land of Oz. Now don't get wrong, his audition was no cake walk, it was a challenge. His dance steps by no means were cutesy, munchkin, or Mickey Mouse like, but rather mature, sexy and cutting edge.

So to make a long story short, I was accepted into the school. Of course I immediately enrolled in Mr. T.'s class. And I soon found out that, no, I wasn't dreaming, his class was always like that. It was always fun. Plus, you could count on his dynamic music and pulsating dance moves to be exhilarating, funky, fresh and current. Yes, his class was like a party. Even though it as well had all the other proper elements we needed too, such as good solid technique, rhythmic challenges, style, and choreographed routines that not only stretched our minds but gave us lots of versatility as well. Believe me, like I stressed before, his was no joke. Mr. T. made us work our little bun buns off. The class really was like a taste of Techno dance "heaven" where each week he opened his "good book." And then he'd flip through the pages to joyously find one of his diverse and mind blowing dance routines that encompassed anything from rock, theatre, contemporary, or whatever style Mr. T. decided to dish out.

It made me love being able to **"Sweat with the Best"** in a room full of amazingly talented dancer/performers five days a week. Okay, now since I'm talking about sweating, I know you didn't think I forgot about Mr. T.'s "No- Sweat Hair do" best kept secret did you? Well I didn't. So this is what I did. I asked a friend of mine whose hair never seemed to get fully wet either. What did he say? He revealed to me that he wore a toupee just like Mr. T.

When he told me this I went into a total state of shock. It was simply because I couldn't believe it. Then I thought, "He wears one too; who would have known?" I mean, it looked so real on them both. However, now I realize these were no ordinary toupees. My guess is they had to be a special brand; possibly top of the line models. Here's why I thought so: the texture and look was so refined that it would have made wealthy tycoons like Donald Trump shout for joy to have one. Simply because this diva brand never once looked out of place, teetered around, nor did it move around back and forth unannounced. I was so surprised this never happened, at least from what I observed while he was teaching class and dancing around. What amazed me was that this never seemed to be a problem for my friend nor Mr. T. I love how it was no big deal to him, but his passion for music and dance was everything to me.

You see, Mr. T. possessed a very special gift. He could put on any piece of music, listen to it several times, and then have a complete routine all figured out. The freaky thing was that he had a knack for hearing musical phases that the normal ear couldn't pick up. It was like he was able to get inside the music and pluck it from the roots. Then the finishing touch would be how he brilliantly made the reflection of the musical piece fit his choreography. For instance, he would associate a series of turns with string instruments and create moves around them that flowed beautifully and melodically. Or he could totally switch the pace by going to a different section in the music that stirred up a more progressive, hard hitting drum section that required sharp dynamic moves. Having such talent was a real motivator. Plus, his love and enthusiasm for dance was so infectious. He could make even the most typical college student having a bad or depressing day, or maybe even low on cash, or any starving artist just passing through, get excited. It was a fact, that if you took his class, he'd make you forget about your worries. Especially once you saw Mr. T. do what we would call," Shimmy Like the Rent is Due." What was it? Check this out!

This is what would happen when Mr. T. would work himself up into a dancing frenzy. So, "Shimmy Like the Rent is Due" is the name we created for this spontaneous burst of energy. This is what would happen. Mr. T. would often get so carried away while creating a dance routine that he'd get lost in the moment, and end up in a world of his own for a wee bit, which would therefore provoke him to go on and on - way past the normal eight counts of eights he taught. It was fun seeing him do this, so immediately when this happened, a crowd would gather around to cheer him on. In fact his class was usually jammed-packed with eager, ready, willing, and waiting students who surrounded him from all four corners of the room. When this happened it meant Mr. T. was on the loose, so stand still and watch with enjoyment. Then be prepared to make a pathway to let him through so he can dance his way through the crowd. Don't go too far away, because afterwards comes your cue to be prepared to duplicate the moves you saw!

It was during this heated moment that Mr. T. worked up a fierce combination of moves. It was like a doctor on an operation table using a number of instruments that zipped, zapped, diced and spliced. I mean these weren't your ordinary run of the mill kind of moves either. These were fiery hot, chest popping, high kicking; booty-shaken concoctions that if drunk in liquid form would make even a witch doctor's hair stand up a little higher on his head. That's why we were so enthralled with anticipation to see what would be the outcome; so we gather around him like the waves on the beach. We would say he was "feeling the spirit." Okay move back, people and let him through the crowd, because he's

about to part the Red Sea! What we meant was, move aside
and let this man through as he twisted and twirled his way
through the crowd to put together another dynamic dance
routine.

Yes, it was truly a joyous occasion. Another unique
characteristic Mr. T. possessed, is that he was always open
for suggestions about what we liked dancing to, and he
encouraged us to bring him pieces of music that inspired us.
If someone took him up on the challenge, he would simply put
the tune on, listen to it a few times, and then - bingo! - come
up with a dance routine right there on the spot. And it made
no difference what style of music it was; pop, hip-hop, or edgy
rock; he could do it all. It was a fact that if "You Gave Him The
Music, He Would Show You The Dance." There's no doubt this
is one of the many attributes that made Mr. T. **"Stand Out and
Stand Apart"** from other instructors. What I know for sure
is, no matter what he did, you could always count on it being
something hot that would make you **"Shimmy Like the Rent
is Due."**

**Here's your Funky Mr. T.'s "Sweat with the Best!" Recap @
Work.**

**(Use These Motivational Groovement Techniques to Help
Empower Your Life)**

* **Do What Feels Right!**
  Step into Your Greatness (Explore)
* **Don't Just Sit Around and Wait For Something to
  Happen Because if That's the Case It Probably Never
  Will! Instead:**
* **Create a New Experience & Do Something Different;
  It'll Bring a Different *Experience and You'll Get
  Different Results!**
* **Fit in Where You Can Get In!**
* **Aim High! Give It Your Best Shot and You Just Might
  Hit the Bulls Eye!**
* **Jazz it Up! Your Passion, Your Spirit & Your life!**

* **Find a Mentor and Believe They Do Have the Magic Touch!**
* **Become Masterful at Whatever You Choose to Do; Trust Me, It'll Show.**
* **Dress the Part and You'll Most Likely Work the Part!**
* **Stand Out & Stand Apart!**
* **Break Through the Crowd!**
* **Concoct Your Own Unique Formula For What You Do! Put Your Spin On It!**
* **Save Up Your Precious Coins (Money) For That Golden Opportunity. Then *Be Prepared to Drop em` Like It's Hot When the Time Comes, and It Will, Okay!**
* **Go Happy & It'll Make You Shimmy Like the Rent is Due!**

Now it's your turn to take the step and make the change that will allow you to Step Into Greatness! Know that doing so will not only be empowering to you, but it will also give others permission to do the same.

You can make a powerful impact on our world just like the companies listed below, whom I personally want to thank for joining me in the continual pursuit to "Perform" by bringing you a standard of excellence. Check out how they "Step Into Greatness!"

TM

World Dance Groove

Step Into Greatness by teaching

you how to "*Live Your Best by*

Training Your Best"

www. youtube. com/worlddancegroove1

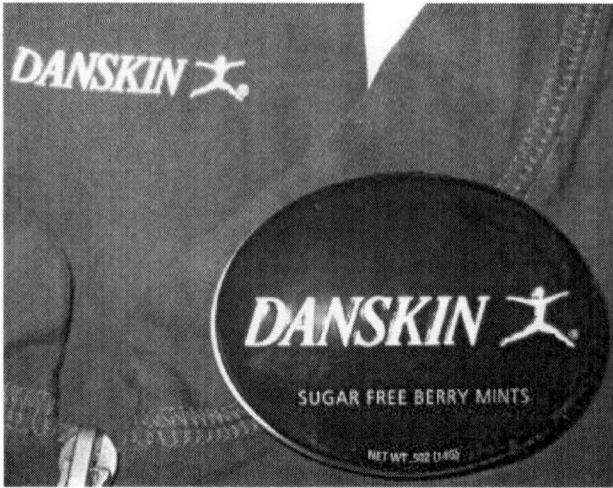

DANSKIN

Step Into Greatness by providing WOMEN with high quality dance/fitness apparel "That Makes Them Feel Good From The Outside In!"

www.danskin.com

Arrowhead

Step Into Greatness by assuring you the purest taste in 100% crisp and clean "Mountain Spring" water.

www.arrowheadwater.com

Step Into Greatness (notes)

Step Into Greatness (notes)

Step Into Greatness (notes)

Step Into Greatness (notes)

Step Into Greatness (notes)

Step Into Greatness (notes)

Step Into Greatness (notes)

Order Now:

**Get Up & Groove (Series)
Motivation Movement Techniques
Presents Book 2**

Be Hot Like Fire
"Start Moving!"

Lightning Source UK Ltd.
Milton Keynes UK
UKOW02f0147270816

281510UK00001B/88/P